The Young Entrepreneur

What YOUNG entrepreneurs can teach ALL people about life, success, and prosperity!

Alyssa Rispoli

Published by Motivational Press, Inc.
2360 Corporate Circle
Suite 400
Henderson, NV 89074
www.MotivationalPress.com

Manufactured in the United States of America.

ISBN: 978-1-62865-050-1

Contents

Acknowledgements

While the keys to success are spelled out in this book, success never happens in a vacuum. The journey to success intersects with others in such a way that life becomes filled with relationships that positively make a difference. While I do not have the pages in this book to thank every person who has positively impacted my journey, I do want to mention some special relationships. First I would like to thank all of the young entrepreneurs who agreed to be featured in this book. Their stories have inspired me and now will inspire millions. Secondly I would like to thank Lindenwood University. Lindenwood is a private Liberal Arts University located in St. Charles Missouri. The education that they have provided me is priceless. Their entrepreneur and business program is top notch and they have educated and supported me on my success journey. Finally I would to thank my Mother and Father. Their love and support has helped shape who I am today.

Preface

From this moment forward you have the choice to do whatever you want with your life. Whether you are young, old, big, or small, it makes no difference. You can stop living your life in the day to day routines of waking up, going to work or school, coming home, and doing it again the next day. You can stop this repetitive lifestyle today. You have the choice, no matter who you are, or where you came from, to become whatever you want to be, and you can make it happen today. You have the opportunity to explore the potential that you hold, in making your life completely different, to be financially free, to go wherever you want, whenever you want. It is a new age, and new times. For instance the internet is rapidly growing, education is becoming more widespread, classrooms are now online, smart phones are in every hand, and technologies are advancing. We are living in a complex world, with a thriving group of young entrepreneurs that are transforming the planet one step at a time. This book is going to teach you the steps to becoming a prosperous entrepreneur, and what young entrepreneurs can teach all people about becoming successful. This book could not have been possible without different technologies like social media, Skype, and email. How else would I have reached young entrepreneurs on the other side of the globe? I have had the chance to be raised in this age of technologies, and this has given myself and many other young entrepreneurs a different outlook on the steps to becoming successful. Yet there is something in common throughout the history of all entrepreneurs, no matter what time period you were raised in, that all entrepreneurs have in common, and that is being able to change your mind set. After reading this book, you will have changed your mindset, and this alone will lead tremendously to your success.

Chapter 1 (The Entrepreneur Mindset)

To start off lets define what an entrepreneur is really all about.

An **entrepreneur** is someone who believes anything is possible, who sees opportunity when others see impossibility, someone who is willing to take risks, is focused, and works hard. An entrepreneur is someone who knows nothing is unrealistic, someone who contributes to something much bigger than his or her own self and is willing to create, learn, and make things happen.

It is never too late to start living a dream. There is no exact way to become successful, but this book will give you some important keys that most successful people follow. There is no class that teaches you step by step what you have to do to become a successful person, or entrepreneur. Entrepreneurship is truly an art, because there are so many ways you can paint your picture, and they can all be great; there is no right and wrong.

"'If you don't do it now you're never going to do it". This is the mentality which you need to start. It is really important to understand that you cannot wait any longer to begin. If you wait, it's not going to happen. You will just keep putting whatever it is off time and time again until eventually it will be forgotten. There are two types of people in this world: those who do, and those who don't. Write down your goals and make them happen. Time is of the essence, and only you are in control of your present and future. You need to live a few years of your life like most people won't, so you can spend the rest of your life like most people can't. People that write down their goals or visions on paper are 75 times more likely to accomplish them. So write! Give yourself time to think, brainstorm, and reflect. The way people live now is that they are constantly on the run, from work, to school, to friends, to family, to everything! People are always coming up with excuses as to why they can't or why they don't have time. Excuses have become some people's biggest flaws. If there is something you want bad enough you will find a way to make time for it. "When you want to succeed as bad as you want to breathe, then you'll be successful" is a quote from a viral youtube video about success by Greyskale Multimedia. Although this quote takes it to the extreme, there is some value to the statement. You have to start somewhere. If you take one hour out of your day to stop and think, whether you just sit there and plan, read, write, to grow internally, that is only

4% of your hectic day. It is also important with crazy hectic schedules to keep yourself healthy. Healthy success is important because the mind and body run together simultaneously. The journey you are about to embark on will not be easy, but it will be worth it. Anything that is worth it usually isn't that simple. If becoming successful was easy then we would all be millionaires. One more tip before we get started is remembering to give. Keep in mind that the window you give through is the same window you receive through, whether you are helping out at charities, donating blood, or opening a door, just consider that in business it is not always about yourself, but something much greater.

Chapter 2 (Upbringing)

Ever since I was a child I have been driven to make money. There is something inside you that drives you to do things, a burning passion, or thought that is always on your mind, and for me this was always making things happen. It all started out when I was very young with lemonade stands and leave raking businesses. When I was 9 years old I wanted some extra cash to buy candy, treats, bikes, and other ordinary 9 year old things. I asked my father to take me to the dollar store down the street from our house. I then asked him if I could borrow 50 dollars. Of course he was a little confused at first, but I promised to pay him back. I took that 50 dollars and turned it into almost 300 dollars in about two hours, when I was only 9 years old. I bought 50 yard sticks, the painted wooden flower that sticks in your yard, and sold them door to door for 5 dollars apiece. If a 9 year old can make 300 dollars in two hours so can you. You need to get creative and think outside of the box. Everywhere you look there is money. Take a moment to look around the room you are sitting in. Everything you see has made money for someone, somehow. It is astonishing to think about everything in this way, but like they always say, there's no such thing as a free meal. If you open up your mind to think about everything in a different way, you will understand that everyone has the potential to make however much money they desire.

As I have gotten older, now 22, I have learned a lot more about sales, marketing, finance, and making money. I have successfully started my own clothing line and advertising company. One tip of advice that I can give from what I have learned in the process of starting my own companies is that one of the best ways to learn is to get out there and do it. I have learned so much more by starting my own companies and getting out there and doing it myself than any class or lecture has ever taught me. I am a young entrepreneur, and I have learned that you have to work hard to play hard, and that's a fact.

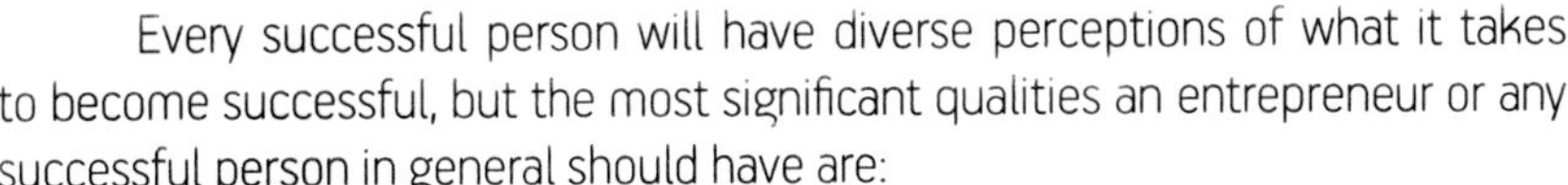

Chapter 3 (Recipes for success)

Every successful person will have diverse perceptions of what it takes to become successful, but the most significant qualities an entrepreneur or any successful person in general should have are:

» **Courage**

» **Determination**

» **Environment**

» **Opportunity**

» **Passion**

» **Action**

These 6 keys are the major reoccurring themes as you read the remainder of this book and meet the young entrepreneurs. These six keys will tremendously contribute to the amount of success you can have in your life. If you follow this guide you will become successful, no doubt, because with courage, determination, enviornment, creativity, and passion, nothing can stop you.

Courage= the eagerness to take risks. Not being afraid of making things happen. One of the keys to success that has helped build accomplishments for many successful people is having the courage to: Start Now! Or as some people say Start Yesterday. This is a crucial step in becoming successful. Many people put great ideas off again and again, and it will never happen this way. You have to start now; this is very important. Even when it comes to investing, developing smart investing practices now will have exponentially greater results in the future because of compounding returns. Even if you are not looking to invest, you can still use this compounding theory with anything that you start now rather than later. The sooner you start the more time you will have to make mistakes, and learn from them. A good idea without action is worth nothing. Having the courage to ask questions is furthermore very important. When you don't know something, just ask. Knowledge is power. You should try to learn as much as you can about everything you do. This will only help you. Right now, there is a lot you don't know. And if you never challenge your own thoughts, the list will never shrink. You will be surprised with what you will learn.

"Formal education will make you a living. Self education will make you a fortune"

Jim Rohn

A man named Josh Whitford spent a lot of time last year working on a business plan involving E-books. He was inspired by Timothy Ferriss's book The 4-hour Workweek: Escape 9-5, Live Anywhere, and join the New Rich. His task was to contact a famous person, and he did. Around Christmastime Josh wrote a simple letter to Warren Buffet, one of the wealthiest men in the world.

Dear Mr. Buffett,

My name is Josh Whitford, and I live in Fargo, ND. I am looking for a bit of advice. There are few things I know better than the fact that I truly do not know much. I do not seek knowledge but rather wisdom. I admire the foresight you have that has led to your success as a person. I would like to know what single piece of wisdom you would offer to someone you have never met.

Sincerely,
Josh Whitford
Seasons Greetings

A couple weeks later Josh received his postcard in the mail. The response was **"Read, read, read"** and nothing more. Josh said, "I do enjoy reading compared to the majority of Americans who only read 1 book a year. I guess you could say that I read 1200% more than the average American. If you haven't read lately, feel free to pick up a book, cozy up on your recliner, crack the spine (of the book that is) and enjoy." This just shows you how important it is to ask questions and to have the courage to do something outside of your comfort zone. This specific response also illustrates the importance of reading. Like Mr. Buffet said, Read, read, read.

The more you learn, the more you realize you don't know, knowledge is addicting, and powerful. **Knowledge is wealth!**

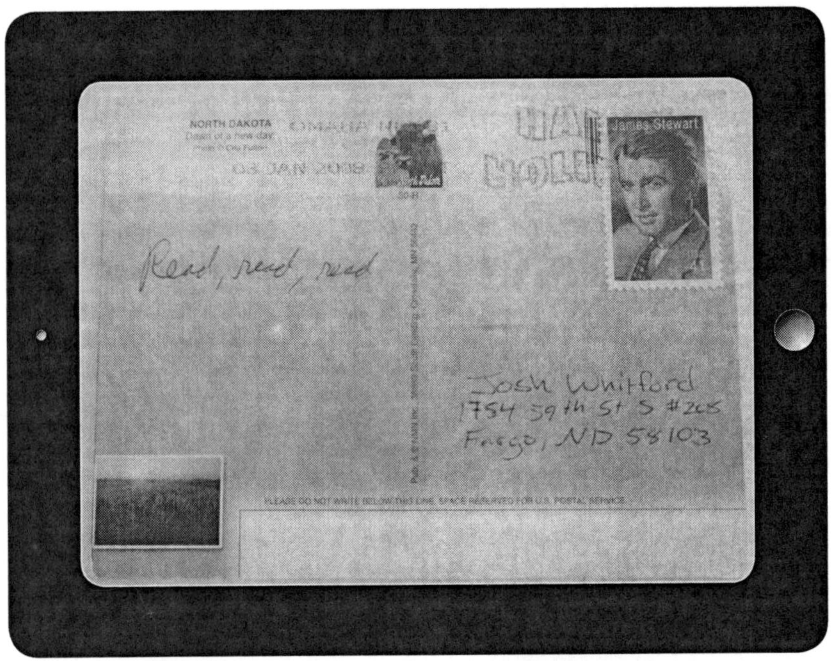

"I'm hungry for knowledge. The whole thing is to learn every day, to get brighter and brighter. That's what this world is about. You look at someone like Gandhi, and he glowed. Martin Luther King glowed. Muhammad Ali glows. I think that's from being bright all the time, and trying to be brighter."

Jay-Z

Determination= the ability to never quit and not give up during hard times. When you fall, you get back up. Successful people look at defeat as an opportunity for success. They are determined to make all of their endeavors succeed; therefore they will try again and again until it works. Mistakes are great instructors; they draw attention to unpredicted opportunity you may have never thought of before. Mistakes are also great learning opportunities and can spark your imagination. Not giving up when you make a mistake or fail is an essential element of becoming successful, in anything that you attempt. Successful entrepreneurs do not believe that something cannot be done.

There is nothing that is impossible.

> ***"Impossible is just a big word thrown around by small men who find it easier to live in the world they were given than to explore the power they have to change it. Impossible is not a fact. It's an opinion. Impossible is potential. Impossible is temporary. Impossible is nothing."***
>
> **Muhammad Ali**

If every time someone told me no, or I couldn't do it, or it was a stupid idea, and I took that to heart and gave up, I would have missed out on tons of opportunities that ended up becoming huge successes. When it comes to becoming successful it is inevitable that you will make mistakes along the way. No matter how smart you are, you will still mess up. You cannot have good ideas unless you are willing to generate a lot of bad ones first. Thomas Edison did not invent the light bulb on his first try. When Thomas Edison was interviewed by a young reporter he audaciously asked Mr. Edison, "Do you feel like a failure and do you think you should just give up by now?" Puzzled, Edison replied, "Young man, why would I feel like a failure? And why would I ever give up? I now know definitively over 9,000 ways that an electric light bulb will not work. Success is almost in my grasp." And shortly after that interview and around 10,000 attempts, Thomas Edison invented the light bulb. You have to be determined. Make the conscious decision that you are willing to do whatever it takes to get the outcome that you desire. Recognize that you only fail when you give up, and no matter what barrier you come across along your journey to success are only learning experiences, that will make you better. As a result failure is not an option. With this state of mind you will have no difficulty accepting that your success is unavoidable.

> ***"Obstacles cannot crush me. Every obstacle yields to stern resolve. He who is fixed to a star does not change his mind"***
>
> **Leonardo Da Vinci**

YOUR SUCCESS IS NOT JUST ABOUT YOU. IT IS ABOUT THE POSITIVE IMPACT YOU GIVE TO THE LIVES THAT SURROUND YOU.

Environment= Surrounding yourself with successful, positive people. Positive attracts positive. Human beings naturally feed off of other people's energy. Have you ever noticed when you are hanging out or working with negative people or people that are all in a bad mood, you tend to be in a bad mood yourself? Surrounding yourself with positive people will release positive energy in your own life. If you surround yourself with people who are successful, driven, ambitious, and positive, you will be much more likely to succeed. As Mark Twain once said, "Keep away from people who try to belittle your ambitions. Small people always do that, but the really great make you feel that you, too, can become great." Get involved with a mastermind group that you can feed off of ideas with one another. Working with a team of people will not only keep you on track, but it will help you generate new ideas. Every successful company and person has worked with other people to make their goals happen. Look at Bill Gates for example; he surrounded himself with other knowledgeable people who all had input in the creation of Microsoft, which is now a multibillion dollar company. Bill Gates had a mastermind team; he did not do it alone. There are many groups like this; you can even find a mastermind team online to join. Another point of creating a successful environment for yourself is learning the law of attraction, and how to use it to influence success in your own life. You are a magnet to the universe, and like I have already said positive attracts positive. You must believe in yourself, and whatever you are doing. The book written by Rhonda Byrne, The Secret, puts the laws of attraction in great understanding and detail. When you change your mind, you can change your world. Changing your mindset is crucial. Stop thinking of the negatives, and think about what you want and how you are going to make it happen, no matter what obstacles come along with it. The power of the mind controls everything. Change your outlooks, and you can control your future.

THERE IS PLENTY OF MONEY ON THE PLANET EARTH; JUST NOT ENOUGH PEOPLE WHO KNOW CORRECTLY HOW TO THINK ABOUT IT, TO BECOME SUCCESSFUL YOU HAVE TO THINK ABOUT MONEY IN A DIFFERENT WAY, AND START VISUALIZING SUCCESS. PICTURE YOURSELF AS VIVIDLY WINNING AND THIS ALONE WILL CONTRIBUTE IMMEASURABLY TO YOUR SUCCESS.

Opportunity= Being able to see opportunities and being able to make links between unrelated events or situations. Seeing opportunity in something when others see nothing is a significant part of becoming successful. Being creative is a big part of being able to see those opportunities when others see nothing. Creativity is something that some people are blessed with and others must learn. But either way you can be creative. In many companies creativity is a key component, and it is what separates them from other companies or products, it is their competitive advantage. Get creative, and create multiple streams of income. Successful people do not just rely on one source of income, they have many.

The story I am going to share with you not only exemplifies the creativity you need to become successful, but it also demonstrates an average person seeing an opportunity that no one else saw, and making a fortune because of that. It is a collection of short stories called The Jakata Tales, which are based on legends of ancient India. While there is no definite date that can be allocated to these tales, it materializes they were assembled between 3rd century B.C. and 5th century A.D. This story is here retold by Raam Anand.

In the city of Varanasi, a young man was once on the lookout for a suitable job. It so happened that the King's Treasurer, accompanied by a friend, passed by.

'The King values your work. The treasury is overflowing with riches. What is the secret of your success?' asked the treasurer's friend.

'Initiative & Enterprise. I'll explain what I mean...' replied the wise treasurer and continued, pointing to a dead mouse on the street...

'Do you see that dead mouse?... Yes?... Even without any money, anyone with initiative could just pick up that mouse and start a business'

'A dead mouse as capital?!!!... Ha..Ha..Ha..' laughed the treasurer's friend and the duo went away.

The young man stopped and gazed at the dead mouse.

'It sounds like an absurd idea... But the treasurer must surely know what he is talking about!' thought the young man and hesitantly picked up the dead mouse.

'But what can I do with it? Who would want to buy a dead mouse?'

'Hey, pussy cat, come back! Ah! Now I know what has attracted him' yelled a man who was passing by with his pet cat.

The cat, attracted by the dead mouse, had jumped out of it's owner's arms.

'My friend, will you sell your mouse to me? I'll pay you one coin for it.' asked the cat owner.

'The mouse is yours!'

'The first coin I've earned!' the young man was excited.

'But what can I do with this small coin?... The wise treasurer has said one must have enterprise...Hmm'

'Oh! I've got it. I must find out if there is a demand for something and then arrange to supply it!' thought the young man and went into a grocery shop...

'Give me one coin's worth of jaggery (sugar) please...'

The next morning, the young man filled a pot with drinking water mixed with jaggery and went to the outskirts of the city.

'I'll wait here for the flower-gatherers to return from work'

In the forest, workers were busy collecting flowers. It was late in the afternoon when they finished their work and began returning to the city.

'It's so hot! and I'm so thirsty! There won't be any water to drink till we reach the city', the workers felt.

'Ah! here they come!...' stood up the young man.

'Brothers, you must be tired. Have some sweet-water...'

'Thank you, friend... May you live long... All we can give you is this bunch of flowers from each one of us. How refreshed we feel after drinking that water! May these flowers also make you happy...'

Each of the workers gulped some water and gave him a bunch of flowers in return. 'Bring us water tomorrow as well, my friend'--the workers left.

The young man took the flowers to the temple in the city. There he sold sold them for eight coins.

With the money he earned, the young man bought a bigger pot and larger quantity of jaggery (sugar).

The next day he went back to the forest to give drinking water to flower-gatherers and even further away, to the fields where grass-cutters were working.

'Is anybody thirsty?'

'You won't find anyone here who is not thirsty. Give me some water, son...' the grass-cutters gracefully drank the sweet-water.

'Brother, you are kind to us. What can we do for you in return?'

'Nothing at present' replied the young man.

'But... don't hesitate to ask us when you need our help'

A month passed by.

One evening, the young man was returning home when a storm broke out.

Everywhere the wind blew down leaves and dry branches.

'If there's money in a dead mouse, there should be money in these leaves and branches, too!'

The next morning he went to the palace garden and spoke to the gardener.

'You look worried, uncle. Can I help you?'

'How can you? The garden is littered with branches... And the King is expected any moment now... I don't know how to clean the mess before he comes' wailed the gardener.

'I'll help you if I can keep the fallen branches' offered the young man.

'Take them, son... Only take them away soon'

'I'll be back in a minute' the young man left the messy garden.

He didn't have to go far to find a group of playing kids.

'Would you like to have some sugar candies?'

'Candies? Oh, certainly!' the kids shouted.

'Then come on, boys. I'll give you some. Everyone will get his share... '

The little kids were happy.

'Would you like to have some more? But you must earn it'

'Tell us what we should do! We are ready!' shouted the excited kids.

'Then come with me. You must collect all the fallen branches in the garden and heap them outside. That's easy! and fun too!'

Quickly they gathered up the fallen branches and heaped them outside the garden. The garden now looked clean and fresh.

'Ah! you have finished! here's your reward, delicious sugar candies! Thank you friends'

Just as the young man was wondering what he should do next... a potter came by and stopped his cart.

'Is that heap of firewood for sale?...'

'Yes of course...'

'Here are sixteen coins. Please help me load my cart. Now I have all the wood I need to fire the pots specially ordered by the King'

The young man then went with the potter to the market.

'Have you heard? The horse dealer will be coming tomorrow' the young man overheard a conversation in the market.

'Yes, yes, I hear he will be bringing five hundred horses to sell'

The young man thought for a minute...

'Aha! that's useful information...'

Hurriedly he went to the grass-cutters and said 'Friends, I seek a favor from you'

'At last! tell us what we should do' replied the grass-cutters.

'I want a bundle of grass from each of you' told the young man.

'We are five hundred in all. So, as many bundles of grass will be delivered to you tonight' the grass-cutters happily agreed.

The young man continued...

'And I want you to promise that till tomorrow afternoon you will not sell anyone any grass at all'

The grass-cutters replied, 'You are our friend. You have given us sweet, flavored water when we were thirsty without getting anything in return. We will do what you ask without question'

The next morning the horse dealer arrived with five hundred horses at the outskirts of the city.

'Strange! no one has come yet to sell me grass for my horses'

He went to the market.

'No grass in a city like Varanasi?'

'Where have all the grass-cutters gone?'

Just then the horse dealer came across the young man's house and saw a big heap of grass bundles.

'Grass! At last! Young man, will you sell all this grass to me? I'll pay you well for it' enquired the horse dealer.

The young man said, 'The grass is yours, Sir'

'Good! then help my man load the cart'

'Here you are Sir, five hundred bundles of grass'

'And here's your payment--one thousand coins'

The young man was excited.

'One thousand coins! I can put these to good use'

A day later...

'Why is it so quiet here today? Is anything the matter?' enquired the young man, while strolling in the city market.

'Everyone is away making preparations to receive the boats that will be arriving tomorrow' replied a passer by.

'Boats... arriving tomorrow?'

An idea flashed like lightning. He bought new clothes and then went to hire a carriage.

'Send the carriage to my house early tomorrow morning. Here's some money as advance'

Very early the next morning, the young man rode in style to the river harbor with his two friends and waited to receive the visiting merchant.

He was, naturally, the first to greet the visiting merchant.

'Welcome to Varanasi'

'I'm happy to meet you, Sir'

The young man continued, 'I want to buy all the merchandise you have brought'

'Right. It's a pleasure to do business with you' replied the merchant.

The merchant quoted a price to which the young man readily agreed and said, 'I need time to arrange the payment. Meanwhile, here's my signet ring as a token of advance and security'

Then the young man set up a small tent and said to his friends, 'When the city merchants come, bring them in with due courtesy'

At day break, a hundred city merchants came to the harbor and met the visiting merchant.

'My friend, we have come to do business with you!'

'I'm sorry, Sir. I've already sold everything' said the visiting merchant.

The city merchants were taken aback, 'When?? To whom??'

'To that young merchant over there' came back the reply.

The city merchants were shocked...

'He's not one of us! We can't let any new persons into our trade or we'll be ruined! We'll lose our precious customers! let's buy him out! We'll make him an offer he can't refuse!' discussed the city merchants.

'All right, let's go to him' they decided.

'Welcome gentlemen! Welcome! Well, gentlemen, have you a proposal to offer?' the young man asked courteously.

'Sir, we would like to buy a share each of the total merchandise. We'll pay you handsomely... thousand gold coins each... That will make it a hundred thousand gold pieces since there are hundred merchants here. But we need all the merchandise--all of it'

Having agreed to the deal, the young man returned home. 'I still have a big amount left after paying the visiting merchant. And I owe it all to the treasurer's wisdom!'

To express his gratitude, the young man went to call on the treasurer, taking half of his profits with him.

'Sir, permit me to present you with these coins as my humble tuition fee for the lesson I learned from you'

'But, I haven't seen you before! Haven't taught you anything!' said the surprised treasurer.

'Yes, you have! I came by all my wealth in four short months, simply by following your teachings' said the young man.

Then he narrated the treasurer the whole story, starting with the dead mouse.

The wise treasurer listened carefully and thought, 'This young man is extraordinarily clever. Just the person I'd choose for my lovely daughter'

So, he married the young man to his daughter and gave him all his family estates and happily said, 'The goddess of success smiles on those who show INITIATIVE and ENTERPRISE. May you always be so fortunate, my son!'

The moral is: Being able to distinguish opportunity when others see nothing (in this case a dead mouse) success comes, even from small beginnings.

SOME OF THE BEST BUSINESS IDEAS TAKE AN EXISTING PRODUCT OR SERVICE AND FIND A NEW USE FOR IT. JUST THINK ABOUT WHAT NETFLIX OR REDBOX HAS DONE FOR MOVIE RENTALS, OR WHAT ITUNES OR PANDORA HAS DONE FOR LISTENING TO MUSIC. YOU DO NOT NECESSARILY NEED A NEW IDEA OR PRODUCT; YOU CAN ALSO MAKE AN EXISTING IDEA EASIER TO USE, MORE CONVENIENT, OR BETTER.

Passion= Finding your passion, and giving it everything you have. If finding your passion is a struggle, here is a question to ask yourself and think about for a minute: if happiness was the national currency, what kind of work would make you rich? What activities make you lose track of time?

A desire or ambition to achieve your dreams and goals is crucial to becoming successful in what you do, no matter what it is, you have to be passionate. Develop a burning desire for success and become ambitious about it. Do not do something just for the money. I have always been taught to do what you are passionate about and money will follow. Without passion you cannot succeed.

"There is no greater thing you can do with your life and your work than follow your passions – in a way that serves the world and you."

-Richard Branson

Action= this is the single most important key to any successful person. A great idea is nothing without action. This step alone will separate those who thrive from those who do not. Do not focus on great ideas, focus on the execution. It does not take a genius idea but a person that is willing to do it, and make it happen, it could even be a dumb idea, but if you implement it and make it happen, you too can become very successful.

> ***"I've missed more than 9000 shots in my career. I've lost almost 300 games. 26 times, I've been trusted to take the game winning shot and missed. I've failed over and over and over again in my life. And that is why I succeed."***
>
> **Michael Jordan**

You can do it. Once you get past your own mental block, of whatever it is that is stopping you. Whether it is your own self telling you that you can't or other people saying, you can't do that, whatever it might be for you, get past this. You need to be (figuratively speaking) like a snow plow, and just dive in and plow through it. No matter who you are there will always be people who will try to bring you down and tell you that you cannot do something, this is inevitable, but the more energy you give these people or these thoughts, the more powerful it becomes. Learn to brush the negative people and comments off. Action is a vital element to success, if you really want it, you can make it happen. Don't let anything stop you. The world is yours. No matter who you are you can have whatever you want, you just have to make it happen, nothing is stopping you but yourself. Get past these mental road blocks and get into action!

> WHEN YOU REACH THE STAGE IN YOUR BUSINESS OR COMPANY THAT YOU NEED TO START HIRING OTHER PEOPLE, THE BEST ADVICE SUCCESSFUL PEOPLE HAVE TO OFFER ON THIS SUBJECT IS TO HIRE PEOPLE SMARTER THAN YOURSELF, AND LISTEN TO THEM. THIS IS IMPORTANT BECAUSE YOU WANT YOUR COMPANY TO THRIVE, AND LET'S FACE IT YOU CAN'T DO IT ALL, SO MAKE SURE YOU HIRE PEOPLE SMARTER THAN YOURSELF THAT CAN CONTRIBUTE TO YOUR COMPANY IN A POSITIVE WAY. THIS BOOK WAS NOT MADE TO TEACH YOU HOW TO RUN YOUR COMPANY BUT HOW TO BE SUCCESSFUL SO WE WILL MOVE ON FROM THIS SIDE NOTE.

Present to Future

"Businessmen must move with the times...the correlation between knowledge and business as the key to success is closer than ever."

Li Ka Shing (Multi Billionaire and considered the richest person in Asia)

From this present moment in time into the future the internet is something that whether you like or not will be flourishing further and more. The internet leaves a huge door open for many business people. Online businesses are bigger today then they have ever been, and will continue to grow. The internet makes the world a much smaller place. There are so many different ways to make money online. By using the internet you are eliminating a local or national sales aspect and creating a global aspect. With nearly 7 billion people in the world, using the internet can help you create greater revenues. Whether people want to accept the fact that the internet is taking over certain parts of our world or not, generations are changing and so is technology. If people don't hop on board with some sort of internet involvement, in years they could be really lost. Use the internet as a way to sell or at least market your business, whether you use facebook, twitter, or yahoo webpages, use something! The internet is an efficient and cheap way to advertise, and if you don't understand how to use it, have someone help you! You don't want to miss out on all the clientele that you could reach by using an online platform.

REMEMBER TO LEARN SOMETHING NEW EVERY DAY. TAKE ADVICE AND LEARN FROM OTHER PEOPLES, NO MATTER WHOM THEY ARE, YOU NEVER KNOW WHAT YOU WILL LEARN. LEARN SOMETHING NEW EVERY DAY.

"Develop a passion for learning. If you do, you will never cease to grow."

Anthony J. D'Angelo

Chapter 4 (The Young Entrepreneurs)

I have done exclusive interviews with over 100 different young entrepreneurs between the ages of 8 and 35. I have narrowed it down to the top 58 to share with you, they have all made money, some millions, by creating their own flows of revenue. Every young person I interviewed was very successful and bright at a young age. The advice and knowledge they gave me can empower everyone with what it takes to become successful, whether you are 15 or 91, it does not matter.

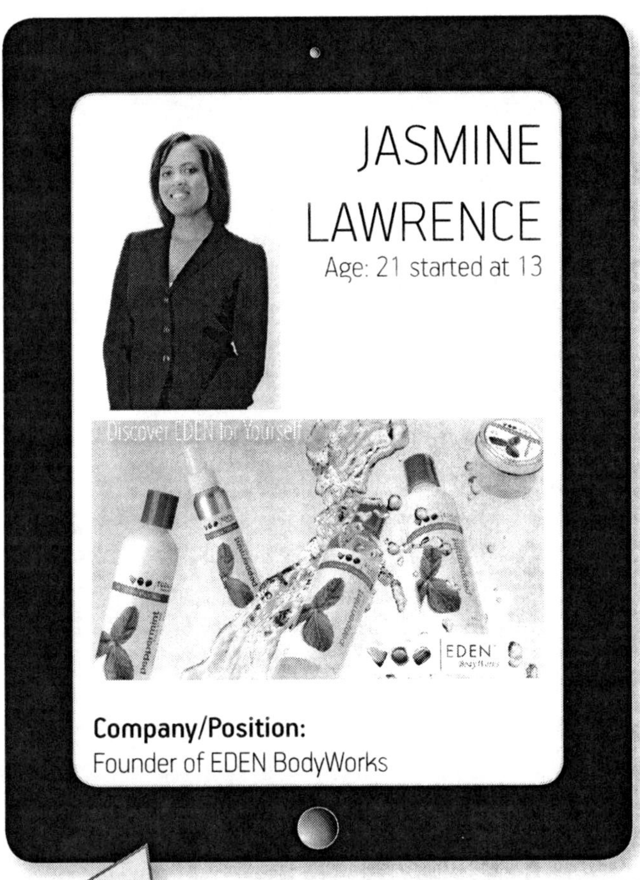

When she couldn't find what she was looking for, this young entrepreneur decided to make her own product. As founder of the company at only 13, Jasmine Lawrence created a company whose revenues are in the millions. EDEN BodyWorks was a huge success; you can even find her products at Walmart. EDEN Body-Works is a hair product line that strengthens and repairs all hair textures whether relaxed, natural, or somewhere in between. Discover softer, stronger, healthier hair with EDEN. EDEN BodyWorks is sold all over the world.

» **Give a detailed description of the work that you do. What are your job responsibilities?**

EDEN Bodyworks creates all natural hair and body care products. My responsibilities are to come up with product ideas and formulations. I also do a lot of promotional events for the company, like speaking engagements and public appearances.

» **What made you think of your idea?**

I started my company at the age of 13 based on a product that I had made for myself. After losing my hair at age 11 to chemicals, I wanted an all-natural solution to help re-grow my hair. I created an all-natural hair oil to help restore my hair.

» **How did you get started?**

In the summer of 2004, I attended a business camp hosted by the Network for Teaching Entrepreneurship. At this camp, I learned all about entrepreneurship and how I could start my own business. When I got home, I used the tools I had learned in the two weeks I spent at New York University to develop a business plan for the product I had made for myself. I first began marketing the product to local hair salons by going door-to-door. In 2006, I launched my website and started selling products online and I got my first distribution contract with Wal-Mart the next year.

» **What were the biggest challenges that you encountered?**

The biggest challenge was gaining respect as a young business woman. There were a lot of people who told me what I couldn't do and how my dream was impossible. Another challenge was learning how to get products into different stores. It was also difficult to balance life as a young teen with the responsibilities of running a company.

» **What would you say is your greatest accomplishment along on the way?**

There are two big accomplishments that stand out. One was the day we realized the company had made 1 million dollars. The second was the first day that my episode on Oprah aired.

» **How did you get into this job? How easy or difficult it was for you to venture into this business?**

It was not hard for me to get into entrepreneurship but to become successful was difficult. It took a lot of hard work and sacrifice.

» **Have you always been interested in this kind of work?**

No, when I was younger my dream was to be an engineer and to build robots. I decided to go to an engineering school after starting my own business so they I could still fulfill that dream.

» **What has this experience been like? Any interesting points you would like to share?**

This has been an amazing experience. I have met people all over the country who have used my products. They tell me what they love and also give me advice on what to do better and new ideas for the future. I am proud that I can support myself financial and even give back to my community. I learned so much about leadership, communication and research over the last eight years. Starting EDEN BodyWorks has really shaped who I am today.

» **What is the most challenging part of your job and why?**

I'm not sure. I really love what I do so I even enjoy the challenges.

» **What fulfillment do you get from your job?**

I love my job! I get to encourage and inspire people to follow their dreams. My products make people's hair and skin healthier and give them self-confidence. It is amazing to see my hard work really helping people.

» **How did you earn your first million? How long did it take? What was your reaction when you realized that you were a millionaire?**

I earned it selling products through my website and at retail stores. Making a lot of money wasn't my objective when I started my business. One of my main goals was to help people around the world. When I made my first million my products were available across the country and EDEN BodyWorks had shipped products to many countries. I was more impressed our global reach than our income.

» **What important lessons have you learned in the process of establishing your company?**

One of the most important lessons that I have learned is how to make a plan. Whenever I want to get something done I can easily analyze the situation and bring people together to accomplish it. I've also learned how to be an effective a efficient leader. I always take my team members opinions into consideration and incorporate their creative ideas with my own. Most importantly I have learned how to manage time. I've learned set priorities and stick to them. I always make time for what is important to me.

» **What do you think helped you the most in your success?**

The Network for Teaching Entrepreneurship was very important to my success. They taught me to be confident and to really think through my business plans. They have continued to support me through mentorship over the years. The support I had from family and friends was also critical. Having a great support system helped me get through rough times and kept me encouraged.

» **Where and how do you see yourself five or ten years from now?**

In the future I see my company product lines greatly expanding. I also see myself pursuing a masters and PhD in engineering. I want to do a lot more traveling to places such as Japan and Australia.

» **How do you spend money – business or personal-wise?**

I don't spend a lot of money. I am very conservative. Most of my personal money goes to eating out with friends or buying computer parts to tinker with.

» **What is the most important advice you would give to other entrepreneurs?**

My advice would be for them to make sure that they are following their passion. Focus and energy are really important to making your business successful and they are hard to fake. They also must know how to communicate their ideas well. In formulating their communication they will be able to think through and challenges or issues that may arise. Entrepreneurs should be forward thinking and open to change.

 www.edenbodyworks.com

 @EDENsjasmine

 www.facebook.com/EDENBlog

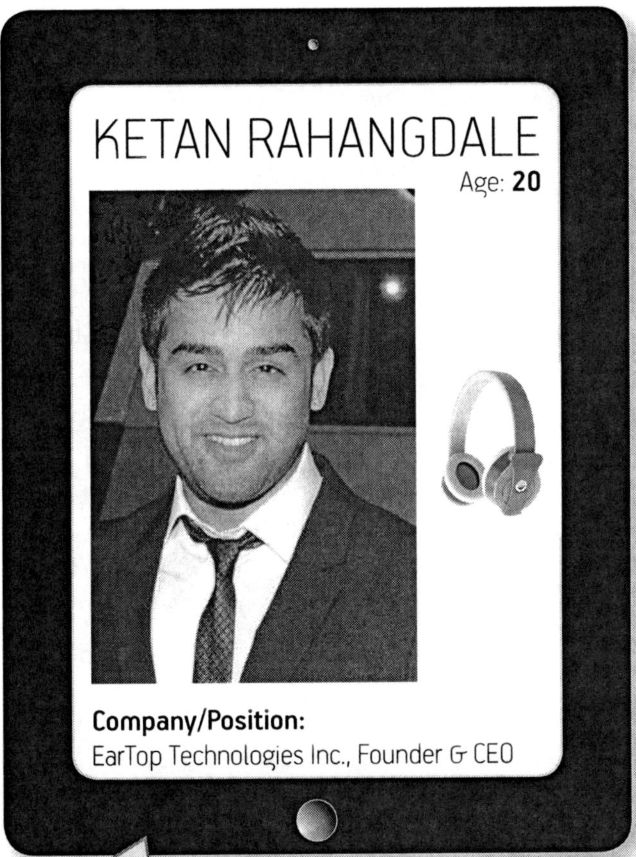

Rahangdale began DJ-ing at parties and concerts at age 12. He decided to create wireless headphones to replace audio cables to make it easier for DJs to set up and maneuver. EarTop Technologies is an audio technology company that designs and manufactures wireless audio and video products. The company's first product is called the Flow Series, which can transform any Beats Solo and Studio headphones and Bose Quiet Comfort headphones into Bluetooth headphones. All it takes is plugging the accessory into the audio inputs on the headphones.

» **Give a detailed description of the work that you do. What are your job responsibilities?**

A large majority of my time is concentrated on developing strategic partnerships, responding to shareholder inquiries, blazing a trail for the future of EarTop, listening and learning from my board of advisors, and setting the general tone of the company.

» **What made you think of your idea?**

DJing. From the age of 13, I had been DJing and around the age of 18 I thought to myself: "Wouldn't it be great if there were high-fidelity, wireless, audio and video-tech products out there?"

» **How did you get started?**

This was quite the process. Before I transferred to the University of Miami, I was privileged enough to live in a community of 21 Entrepreneurs at Babson College. I learned many team building and cooperation skills via these individuals, and it was through going to Elevator Pitch competitions that I began to expand my network.

» **What were the biggest challenges that you encountered?**

Raising capital, and being young. Sometimes, being young worked to my advantage, however when it came to raising Angel and VC funding, the lack of industry experienced was always frowned upon. Less Learned: If you're a young entrepreneur looking to raise any amount of capital, make sure that there is a season veteran on your advisory and director boards, if not a partner in the company itself. While young individuals often times bring great value to a team through diversified skill sets, there is nothing that speaks better to an investor than, "I've been there, and done it before." You get that from the older guys and girls.

» **What would you say is your greatest accomplishment along on the way?**

Building relationships and expanding my network is probably the most valuable accomplishment to date. Hitting revenue milestones, expanding the team, and establishing a brand is all wonderful, however it is the people that I have forged relationships with that I know I can depend on even if EarTop someday vanishes which is really a great accomplishment to me. Also, knowing that I have made a significant impact in the world of audiophiles feels phenomenal. Being in Entrepreneur, FastCompany, Inc., Mashable, and other media is pretty cool too.

» **How did you get into this job? How easy or difficult it was for you to venture into this business?**

Extremely difficult. Unlike most startups out there, going into hardware has its distinct disadvantages in the beginning: It requires a large amount of upfront capital, a tremendous amount of effort to build a solid team, and an even larger effort to compete with long established players in the market. Having said this, I got into this industry because it is my passion. I have loved all kinds of music from an extremely early age, and working in my grandfather's transforming manufacturing company inspired me to make a physical product of my own in an industry of my liking.

» **Have you always been interested in this kind of work?**

Not necessarily. I've loved music, that's for sure. But when I started EarTop I never went into it thinking we would become mass designers and manufacturers of products. I just wanted to create something that I could use personally. When I realized others were extremely interested in the concept, was when I really got interested myself and began to grow into a company.

» **What has this experience been like? Any interesting points you would like to share?**

The experience has been like none other. Being a guy, I almost feel like I know what it feels like to have a child... almost. Creating value in an environment through my company is like creating a baby that grows up to do big things. I'm extremely proud of my accomplishments to date, and I hope my child/company continue to grow to do bigger and better things. One experience I found extremely valuable was when I was at the Kairos Society summit on the NYSE. Here, I learned that building relationships with people through trust and honest work ethic is the most important thing when doing business.

» **What is the most challenging part of your job and why?**

There are many challenging aspects of my job. Managing all constituents of a company from employees, to partners, to directors, to investors is hard enough in itself, not to mention the continual quest to come out with products which can expand upon my vision for the company. But instead of looking at these challenges as a detriment to expediency, I have fun going through these loopholes as I am working on something I am passionate about, and it is incredibly fun.

» **What fulfillment do you get from your job?**

A sense of impact. My goal in life is to impact everyone I can in the world. Through EarTop, I not only get to do something I love, but also impact many people in world, which feels phenomenal.

» **How did you earn your first million? How long did it take? What was your reaction when you realized that you were a millionaire?**

I made my first million through EarTop's first product. It took about a year and a half. I had virtually no reaction when I was a millionaire as all the money I made I re-invested into the company as I want it to continue to thrive and grow to its maximum potential.

» **What important lessons have you learned in the process of establishing your company?**

Trust is the fundamental basis of business. Without integrity no deal will work. Also, a great business deal is not when you win because you think you have a good deal. A great business deal is when you and the other party wins, and you both walk away with a smile on your faces.

» **What do you think helped you the most in your success?**

My team members and networking ability. I have never heard of a shy entrepreneur. In order to grow your business, you must foster new relationships, and it is through expanding your network and having that ability to communicate with others that you will succeed.

» **Where and how do you see yourself five or ten years from now?**

Where will I be? Who knows. However, I know that I hope to be doing exactly what I'm doing but on a larger scale-- that is, being an entrepreneur and being a mover and shaker in the world.

» **How do you spend money – business or personal-wise?**

Life is short. Business wise, don't waste a single penny unless you have to. Personally, give up everything you have to make your business a success. Then, when you're raking in the millions (or billions), give yourself enough of a salary to keep yourself happy and do the things you want to do.

» **What is the most important advice you would give to other entrepreneurs?**

EXECUTE, EXECUTE, EXECUTE! It isn't your genius idea that will create a great company. It is your ability to communicate with others, have integrity, build a team, and then execute on a genius idea that will make you a success.

 www.eartop.com

 @eartop

 www.facebook.com/EarTop

SHRAVAN & SANJAY KUMARAN

Age: Shravan is 12 & Sanjay is 10

Company/Position:
CEO's & Founder's of Go Dimensions

These two brothers, **Shravan** and **Sanjay** Kumaran, are the youngest CEO's in India. These brothers are interested in building applications for educational development and fun by making it a memorable experience for users. They aim to bring convenience and low prices to all their customers. The Kumaran brothers have launched their own mobile applications firm called Go Dimensions.

» **Give a detailed description of the work that you do. What are your job responsibilities?**

We develop apps; we are currently developing Apps for iPhone & Android devices. So far we have built 6 for the iPhone and 3 on the Android. We both develop the apps and we have setup our own company. Shravan Kumaran is President and Sanjay Kumaran is CEO.

» **What made you think of your idea?**

Regarding setting up the company we always wanted to setup our own company, when we developed apps and were going to upload them onto the AppStore, we decided to do it through our own Company and brand rather than as individuals.

» **How did you get started?**

We have been learning programming and playing with computers for quite some time. More than 6 years now. We love computers and have taken on programming. We love playing games on mobile phones, so we thought why not develop games ourselves.

» **What were the biggest challenges that you encountered?**

Not as such any major challenge but getting the App readied for the AppStore and getting iPhone to certify and approve is a great feeling.

» **What would you say is your greatest accomplishment along on the way?**

We are quite happy that our apps are used by our customers in more than 45 countries. When someone says our App was helpful or they enjoy our App it gives us lot of satisfaction. We were thrilled when ex. President of India, Dr.Abdul Kalam mailed us and wished us.

» **How did you get into this job? How easy or difficult it was for you to venture into this business?**

As we said we always wanted to start on our own. Since mobile platform gives freedom to Small business folks with no investment on distribution it was easy for us to position our Apps.

» **Have you always been interested in this kind of work?**

Yes all along.

» **What has this experience been like? Any interesting points you would like to share?**

It has been a wonderful experience so far. We also have been speaking to many college & school students, a few students from India's top schools told us we have inspired them to start their own venture rather than looking for job, we felt really good.

» **What is the most challenging part of your job and why?**

Finalizing an idea and giving it a shape of what we think will be useful for our customers is challenging.

» **What fulfillment do you get from your job?**

We feel quite happy when we see our Apps used by customers and when we see review comments we feel quite happy.

» **What do you think helped you the most in your success?**

We think our faith in God and blessing from family and friends.

» **Where and how do you see yourself five or ten years from now?**

We would like to have our brand established as one of a valued company. Our Vision is to have half of the world's smart phones running our apps.

» **How do you spend money – business or personal-wise?**

The money that we have got from Ads so far we have used to buy gifts for our Parents. Our plan is to give 15% of our profit to poor kids and we are doing that.

» **What is the most important advice you would give to other entrepreneurs?**

Believe in your idea and yourself.

 www.godimensions.com

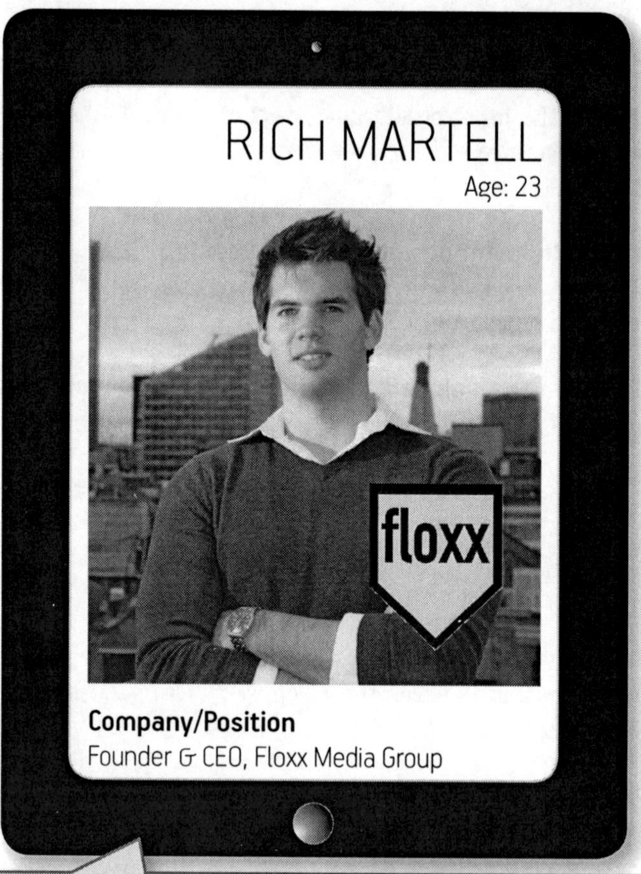

Rich started his first business when he was just 15. Rich is an internet entrepreneur best known for founding Floxx Media Group, being the creator of FitFinder and business expert on the television series Million Dollar Intern. Rich is the founder and CEO of Floxx Media Group. Floxx Media Group is a digital media agency based in London, United Kingdom that specializes in producing mobile apps.

» **Give a detailed description of the work that you do. What are your job responsibilities?**

Being CEO isn't as glamorous as it sounds. You're often the hardest working person in the company, first in, last to leave. When you initially start up you find that your job responsibilities are so wide ranging. You are the chief salesperson, head of product, head of marketing. As you grow you may be fortunate enough to fill these rolls with actual people allowing you to concentrate on the vision. My day to day responsibilities are meeting new clients, working on the initial ideas for apps, meeting our shareholders and investors and finally, recruitment.

» **What made you think of your idea?**

The origins of Floxx stem back from my time as a student at UCL. I was bored in the library one day and decided to set up a website which allowed people to share when hot guys and girls came into the library. I called it FitFinder and it went viral. Within 4 weeks we had 250,000 users across 53 universities. Unfortunately it got shut down by my university but that is what gave me the little taste of the power of the web.

» **How did you get started?**

I've always had an interest in business but Floxx is my first business that I've been able to work on full time (the others were all worked on as I was studying). It's quite odd looking back as I can remember my first day working on it full time. The company was just me, it was 7am and I had a laptop. I had a big long todo list and I just worked my way through it. That todo list is still growing but now I have 10 or so people helping me get through it!

» **What were the biggest challenges that you encountered?**

Raising investment is always a challenge. We've been lucky enough to meet some great investors and have convinced them to buy into Floxx and join us on the journey. Raising investment is a very distracting process so make sure you prepare enough for it so that you can achieve what you set out to achieve in the time you want without it distracting too much from your core business.

» **What would you say is your greatest accomplishment along on the way?**

I've been very proud of building the team we have. We've got some awesome people at Floxx and it's a genuine pleasure working with them day to day. Our brand as a cool, young, vibrant place to work helps us attract top talent when they could easily go and work for a management consultancy or a bank.

» **How did you get into this job? How easy or difficult it was for you to venture into this business?**

I kind of stumbled into this. My plan was always to leave anywhere I worked as an employee to run my own business – it just happened a lot sooner that I thought. It's always a challenge setting up something but I can't imagine anything more rewarding that growing a business from scratch. I plan to do this for the rest of my life!

» **Have you always been interested in this kind of work?**

I've always been interested in technology as a whole. I grew up in the 90's when email and home computing was first being introduced to the masses. I can remember my Dad buying a Time computer which I spent a lot of my youth on and that's when I learnt to program computers.

» **What has this experience been like? Any interesting points you would like to share?**

Running a startup is like no other experience. There are so many ups and downs that you have to be extremely mentally strong. There is a famous saying that entrepreneurs are never happy – this is because they always want progression and sometimes you have to take a step back to make two steps forward. My main piece of advice is to choose something that you enjoy. If you enjoy your work then it won't feel like work. I'd still do this without being paid and of course there are times that are challenging but that comes with the job and you have to get through them.

» **What is the most challenging part of your job and why?**

Making time for everything and everybody is my toughest challenge. As we've grown there are more people to see and catch up with. I find that a large part of my job is making sure I get around seeing what everyone is working on and help them with any challenges they have. I've found it tough to say no to things like casual coffees that more often than not have no benefit. Instead I now have to prioritize my 18 hours a day that I have for work.

» **What fulfillment do you get from your job?**

Starting a company is like have a child (I imagine). It's amazing how much fulfillment you can have by seeing your company grow and develop into a bigger and more productive place.

» **How did you earn your first million? How long did it take? What was your reaction when you realized that you were a millionaire?**

This aspect of things is not something I think about on a day-to-day basis. Sometimes when you raise investment you look at the valuation being placed on you and you can see what value your stake is and sometimes that's scary but I don't feel like that should ever be the main driver. You have to be passionate about what you do and if you set out to disrupt then wealth is a byproduct of this.

» **What important lessons have you learned in the process of establishing your company?**

My biggest lesson is: make sure you hire the right people. Not just the right people but at the right time. We've made a few mistakes by hiring the right people at the wrong time and also the wrong people in general. It's not an irreversible mistake but make sure you try and right your wrong as soon as possible to not hurt your business.

» **What do you think helped you the most in your success?**

Being passionate. I can't stress how much you better you will perform if you are genuinely obsessed with your work. You have to wholeheartedly believe in what you are doing and be prepared to work on it 100%.

» **Where and how do you see yourself five or ten years from now?**

I see myself still running businesses. I'd like to be involved with a few other companies which are in areas I'm interested in like skiing and running. I've got some more ideas which I want to try and get off the ground but the time is not right now. I'd also like to be in a position to angel invest and offer some guidance to young entrepreneurs coming through the ranks.

» **How do you spend money – business or personal-wise?**

I'm usually pretty tight with money. I keep a track of all of my personal and business expenses in a spreadsheet and every few months I analyze them. I find it comforting that I know where I stand with things financially. The main things I do spend money on are my apartment and travelling.

» **What is the most important advice you would give to other entrepreneurs?**

Be prepared to fail. Failure is not a bad thing so long as you learn from it. Every day I fail at something and so far I've been able to learn for the next time around. Often it's tough to face that but the odds are stacked massively against you when you startup. You almost have to remove that emotional stigma attached to failing and view the failure as the success of disproving a hypotheses that you had. Work hard, get 6 hours of sleep a night and exercise!

www.richmartell.com

@RichMartell

www.facebook.com/floxxdotcom

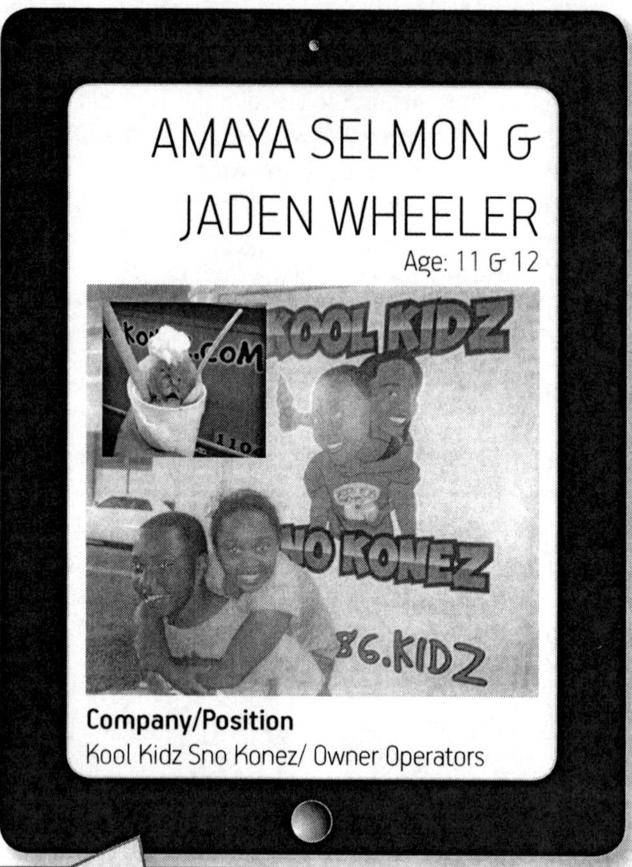

Kool Kidz Sno Konez is a food truck business that was started by two young entrepreneurs. Jaden Wheeler and Amaya Selmon are the youngest owners of a food truck business in Tennessee. The brother and sister team own and operate Kool Kidz Sno Konez, a little enterprise that started in their front yard two years ago and is now flourishing.

» **Give a detailed description of the work that you do. What are your job responsibilities?**

We are a licensed food truck, serving sweet, refreshing sno konez, juicy hot dogs, and yummy nachos!

» **What made you think of your idea?**

In 2011 at age 9 and 10, we were brainstorming of things we could do to make our own money to buy toys and games when we wanted to. At first I wanted to do a yard service but my mom said that was too dangerous. Amaya wanted to do a lemonade stand but i knew that wouldn't make enough money. One day our mom took us out shopping and we stopped to get snow cones at this place across town. The line was soooo long. That's when Amaya and I both looked at each other and said "sno konez!"

» **How did you get started?**

We started our business in our front yard. We set up a folding table, a blender, a bag of ice, and some flavors my mom bought at a nearby grocery store. Our snow cones were priced at 50 cent and $1.00. They were a hit with the neighborhood. The next year, we convinced all of our friends to go out to the main street by our house to hold up sno kone signs and flag customers in. Our sales picked up a whole lot! There were people coming by when we weren't even home. The police officers on patrol would stop by and ask for sno konez. That's when we asked our mom could we start a real business.

» **What were the biggest challenges that you encountered?**

The biggest challenge has been working the glitches out in our truck along the way. Also, now that school is back in, managing our time between school work and business. But we think, we've got that mastered now.

» **What would you say is your greatest accomplishment along on the way?**

Our greatest accomplishment was actually bringing this idea to life. Also we hit a record for our business on August 2, by serving 1000 customers in 4 hours.

» **How did you get into this job? How easy or difficult it was for you to venture into this business?**

The venture has not been that hard. Our mom has been a really big help in supporting us.

» **Have you always been interested in this kind of work?**

No, just the last 2 years of our lives.

» **What has this experience been like? Any interesting points you would like to share?**

This has been an awesome experience! We feel proud to own our own business and our friends think it's the coolest! We have a waiting list for those interested in working with us.

» **What is the most challenging part of your job and why?**

Prepping for big events. Selling sno konez looks easy but there is a lot of work behind the scenes.

» **What fulfillment do you get from your job?**

We feel proud to own our own. It makes us feel good to serve our own community and to be role models for kids our age, representing our generation in a positive light for a change.

» **What was it like when you realized you made your first million?**

We haven't made it there yet. But when we do..FREE sno konez for everyone!

» **What important lessons have you learned in the process of establishing your company?**

We've learned not to give up. If we would have given up at the first hurdle, we would have been done a long time ago. Owning your own business takes a lot of hard work and persistence. Everyone is not going to believe in you and support you, and that's okay. That won't break you. But if you don't believe in yourself, then it's over. You have to have a solid plan and stick to it. Set deadlines to get things done. Once you have reached one goal, set another.

» **What do you think helped you the most in your success?**

Guidance from our mom. Also, letting EVERYONE know what we were doing. Our community has been very supportive, from building apps for us, making t-shirts, getting us media coverage, to booking us for big events.

» **Where and how do you see yourself five or ten years from now?**

Five years from now, I (Jaden) will be in entering my freshman year in college and Amaya will be in 11th grade. By this time, we will have franchised our sno kone business spanning the southeastern portion of the United States. We will also expand with an apparel company and kids' party company. Ten years from now, we would like to franchise internationally, starting with South America and the Caribbean.

» **How do you spend money – business or personal-wise?**

Business wise most of our money goes to SUGAR! (We mix our own flavors) We also have a lot of maintenance on our truck. Personally, we save about 70% of our profit and spend the rest on entertainment, games, and clothing/shoes.

» **What is the most important advice you would give to other entrepreneurs?**

Find something you like and would have FUN doing. If it's something boring to you or you absolutely hate doing it, you will never be successful. Also, don't give up at what seems like your first failure. If you keep going, things will smooth out perfectly.

www.koolkidzsnokonez.com

@koolkidzsno

www.facebook.com/KoolKidzSnoKone

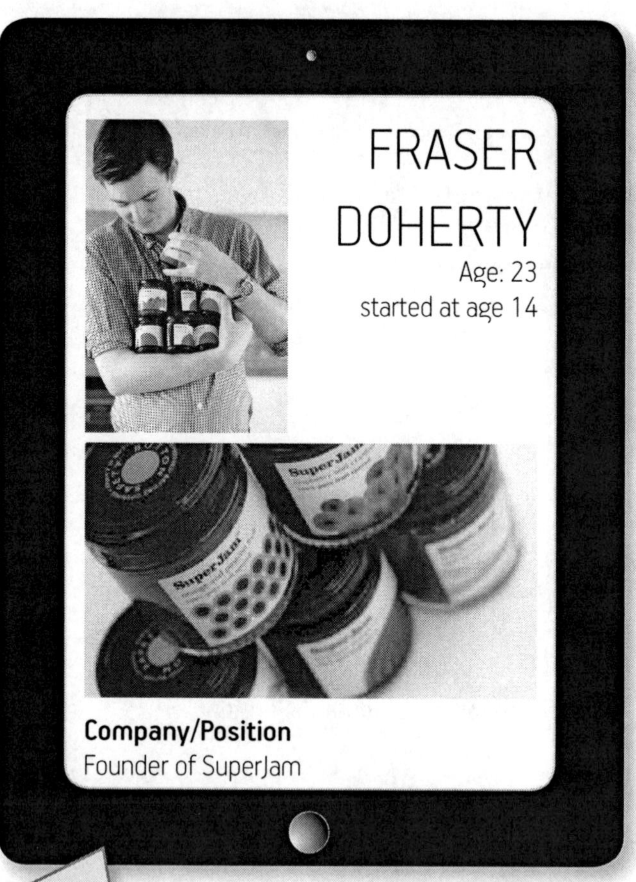

When Doherty was 14 years old he started making jams from his grandmother's recipes in Edinburgh, Scotland and by 16, he left school to work on his jams full time. SuperJam™ is a range of 100% pure fruit jams; sweetened with grape juice and made using Super Fruits, such as blueberries and cranberries. SuperJam was created by Scottish jam-maker Fraser Doherty, after being taught to make jam using his Gran's secret recipes at the age of fourteen. From humble beginnings, the company has gone on to sell millions of jars, has won a variety of awards and is even exhibited in the National Museum of Scotland as an example of an 'Iconic Scottish Food Brand'.

» **Give a detailed description of the work that you do. What are your job responsibilities?**

I'm the founder of SuperJam! We make 100% fruit jams and sell them to thousands of supermarkets around the world.

» **What made you think of your idea?**

I was first taught to make jam by my grandmother at the age of fourteen – I always loved jam and thought it would be amazing if I could make a living out of doing something I enjoy.

» **How did you get started?**

I first began by cooking jam in my parents kitchen at home, selling it to the neighbors and at farmers' markets – it just grew and grew from there.

» **What were the biggest challenges that you encountered?**

I first pitched my products to supermarkets when I was 16 – I turned up wearing my Dad's suit and without any money, experience or clue about how supermarkets and factories worked – I just had an idea that I believed in. It was very hard to convince a factory to work with me, to create a brand and to get a supermarket to agree to put my products onto their shelves.

» **What would you say is your greatest accomplishment along on the way?**

For me, the proudest moment of all was the day that I was able to go into a supermarket, Waitrose, and buy a jar of my own jam – which I did, and stuck the receipt up onto my bedroom wall!

» **How did you get into this job? How easy or difficult it was for you to venture into this business?**

I started on such a small scale that it was easy to get started – I always say, don't think that you have to jump in at the deep end – just dip your toe into the water by giving your idea a shot and you never know where it might take you!

» **Have you always been interested in this kind of work?**

I have always loved cooking but also ever since I was a small kid I saw starting a business as a way that I could have a positive impact on the world.

» **What has this experience been like? Any interesting points you would like to share?**

It has been an amazing adventure – I have been invited to downing street to have dinner with the prime minister, visited over forty countries around the world and even seen my brand, SuperJam, included in the National Museum of Scotland as an example of an 'Iconic Scottish Brand'!

» **What is the most challenging part of your job and why?**

The most challenging thing in life for anyone is probably motivating yourself to keep getting up, trying and trying, especially when things don't work out first time around.

» **What fulfillment do you get from your job?**

As well as seeing SuperJam become a commercial success, it has been great for me to be able to use some of the profits that we have made to give back to the community – over the past few years, we have run hundreds of free tea parties for elderly people who live on their own or in care homes.

» **What important lessons have you learned in the process of establishing your company?**

I've learned that everything takes longer than you first think!

» **What do you think helped you the most in your success?**

I was fortunate enough to have a mentor, a guy called Kevin, who gave me a huge amount of advice and support in about starting my business.

» **Where and how do you see yourself five or ten years from now?**

I tend not to think too far ahead but I am definitely ambitious to see SuperJam grow – we're launching in the US in 2013, which I am very excited about.

» **How do you spend money – business or personal-wise?**

For me, starting a business has never been about trying to get rich. I have been lucky enough to get to travel a huge amount, making friends all over the world along the way – which, for me, is the most fulfilling thing to spend my money on.

» **What is the most important advice you would give to other entrepreneurs?**

Start small. You don't need to borrow lots of money, just test your idea on a small scale and, if it works, scale up organically from there. Find a mentor. Someone who has been there and done it before who can give you advice. Don't be afraid. I meet so many people who have an idea for a business but are just too afraid of taking the first steps and giving it a shot – which is a real shame.

www.superjam.co.uk

@fraserdoherty

www.facebook.com/pages/SuperJam/20413114175

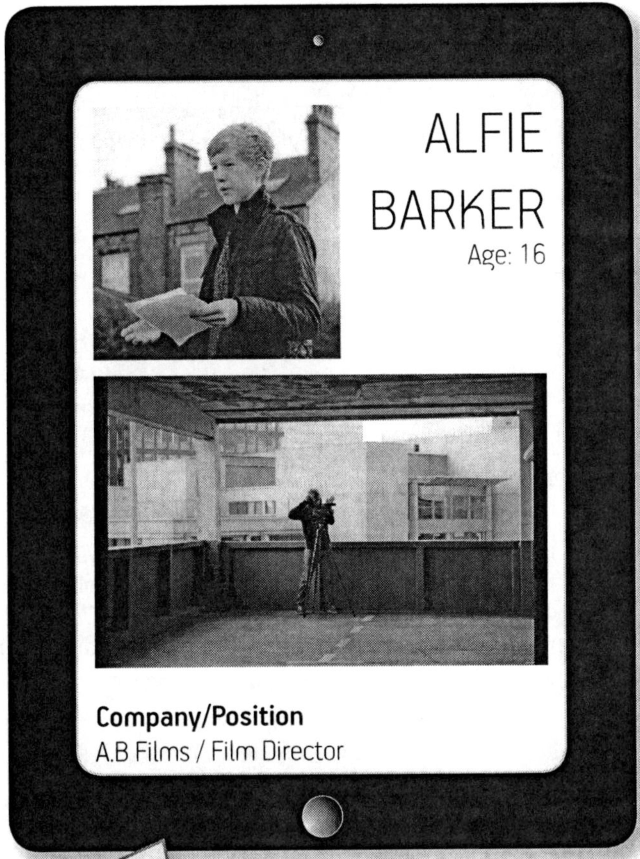

Alfie Barker is one of the youngest film directors in the world. Alfie started making his own films since he was 8 years old. Alfie is pursuing a career in film at a very early stage in his life. He is a multi award winning film director, and has created amazing works.

» **Give a detailed description of the work that you do. What are your job responsibilities?**

I'm currently a student – so technically not actually working although I don't think I would describe my passion of filmmaking as 'working' anyway, more of a hobby I enjoy.

» **How did you get started?**

Since I can remember I have been enthusiastic about art and film with one of my greatest achievements being at an early age when I entered a national competition to paint Rafael's Madonna in the Pinks. I was chosen from hundreds of entries as a winner and had my painting exhibited in The National Gallery, London. Having my award presented by Peter Blake gave me the opportunity to talk to a recognized artist about his work and was a meeting I have never forgotten. In 2004, I made my first film when I was 8 years old after taking part in a stop- motion animation workshop in Leeds, inspired by Wallace and Gromit. Nick Park saw one of my films and wrote to me saying how much he enjoyed it, this has made me even more determined to make films.

» **What were the biggest challenges that you encountered?**

I don't think I've yet encountered any big challenges in my life so far but if there was one thing I'd be challenged by, it would be my age and the restrictions I have when collating a cast, crew and hiring places to film.

» **What would you say is your greatest accomplishment along on the way?**

In November 2011, I won the AXA Ambition Award for the Arts Category, in which I won a large bursary for film mentoring and equipment. The winners were announced in the Royal Courts of Justice, hosted by Carol Vorderman (UK PRESENTER) and presenter for the Arts Category, Alex James (Blur guitarist).

» **What has this experience been like? Any interesting points you would like to share?**

Life changing – shows that you should grab every opportunity you can to succeed because a key point someone once told me was: 'You can get into contact with anyone in the world through 6 people'. It's about who you know what you know – well certainly in my industry.

» **What fulfillment do you get from your job?**

The sense of achievement when I've finished making a short film – it usually shows me that all the hard work pays off!

» **Where and how do you see yourself five or ten years from now?**

I'd like to see myself working on feature films but who knows where life could take me, I hope that one day I'll have made a successful film!

» **What is the most important advice you would give to other entrepreneurs?**

You have to be passionate, if you're not – then not to be too dis-heartening but it won't work. You can find time for anything: if you really want it.

www.alfiebarker.com

@alfie_barker

www.facebook.com/alfiebarkerfilms

Born in Columbia Santiago started his first business when he was only 7 years old, a water delivery business. Santiago has started many businesses throughout his years and it makes sense that he turned down job offers from companies like Google after graduating as his class valedictorian. He instead decided to focus on growing his own company full time. BlueBridge Digital has taken mobile app development to a whole new level. Instead of one-time products, they build partnerships with clients to build, maintain and optimize their apps. They specialize in three types of industries: tourism, higher education, and churches.

» **Give a detailed description of the work that you do. What are your job responsibilities?**

I am the CEO and co-founder of BlueBridge Digital, based out of Fishers, Indiana. I started the company about 2 years ago, and my daily responsibilities include CEO-ing and overseeing our app development brands that cater to city tourism departments, churches, and colleges. I've found "CEO" to be a pretty broad job title, because my role is in constant flux! My time is divided between accounting, development, project management, sales and marketing, while keeping everyone within those areas motivated.

» **What made you think of your idea?**

BlueBridge Digital was born from the belief that there needed to be an easier, smarter way for companies and communities to harness the power of the mobile revolution, and was named for the Blue Bridge ferry boat in New Zealand, where I had an amazing travel experience in college.

» **How did you get started?**

The path that led to my career today has actually bridged (pun intended) several continents and various industries. I first dabbled in entrepreneurship at the age of seven selling water to neighbors in Colombia. After relocating to the US, I started a few small businesses like music camps for kids (MyMusicCamp.com), and University Storage. I didn't have any experience in tech until I was hired as a Slingshot intern with ExactTarget in college. I had an amazing internship experience there and was offered a part-time role while I was still in school. After choosing to study abroad in Australia and through a series of unfortunate events (just like the books), I dropped out of my study abroad program and was fortunate to be hired on as a Partners Associate out of ExactTarget's Sydney and Melbourne offices. After doing business in Australia and New Zealand, the idea to start a tech company manifested itself, and BlueBridge was born right before I started my senior year of college.

» **What would you say is your greatest accomplishment along on the way?**

Creating a business that gives people jobs they enjoy.

» **How did you get into this job? How easy or difficult it was for you to venture into this business?**

Entrepreneurship has been a huge part of what makes me who I am, even from a young age. My first encounter with the technology industry was during my internship at digital marketing agency Exact Target, but once I discovered that the Software as a Service model, though well-established, had never before been applied to mobile apps, I knew I had found a golden opportunity. Before long, the company pivoted to a product model, and in doing so, BlueBridge Digital became a pioneer in the field of Mobile Apps as a Service.

» **What is the most important advice you would give to other entrepreneurs?**

The best career advice, I think, is found in a quote by L.P. Jacks. He talks about how a truly fulfilled life isn't about compartmentalizing or musing on work/life balance. A fulfilled life is about embracing all of life, together, and passionately loving what you do and who you do it with. He writes: "The master in the ART of living makes little distinction between his work and his play, his labor and his leisure, his mind and his body, his information and his recreation, his love and his religion. He hardly knows which is which. He simply pursues his vision of excellence at whatever he does, leaving others to decide whether he is working or playing. To him he's always doing both."

 **www.bluebridgedigital.com**

 **@santiagojara**

 **www.facebook.com/BlueBridgeDigital**

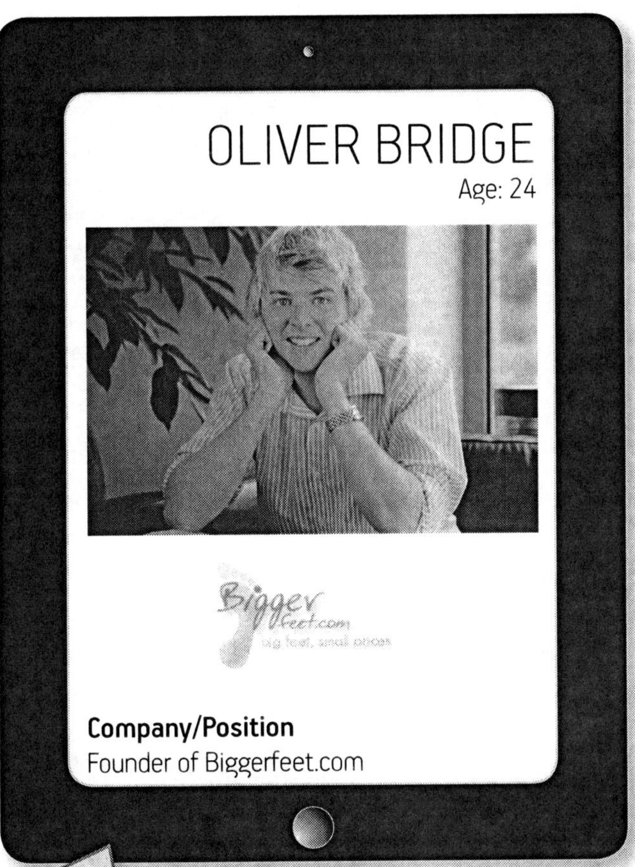

Having big feet himself, Oliver realized the need for a shoe company that offered larger shoe sizes. He saw a gap in the market and created his company at age 16. Biggerfeet offers a wide range of plus size shoes for a reasonable price. Having struggled to find size 13 shoes for himself, Oliver realized that there was a gap in the market for people who needed big shoes. After researching the market by visiting trade shows and meeting manufacturers, it soon became apparent that there was the means to launch a big footwear company as well as the demand.

» **Give a detailed description of the work that you do. What are your job responsibilities?**

I started Bigger Feet – a website for people with large feet – we sell large shoes. I have large feet myself and realized on holiday once that it was difficult to find suitable footwear, so noticed a gap in the market. My mum persuaded me to give it a go, and after £2500 investment, I was ready to go! Today, I have stepped back from the business, and work in the venture capital industry, but my mum continues to run the business. When I was involved in the day to day running, I would do everything from web design through to customer service and doing the accounts – running a business is fairly hands on exercise!

» **What made you think of your idea?**

I was trying to buy some football boots but couldn't get any in size 13! I did some Google research and found out that there wasn't really much available, so I thought there was probably an opportunity to make some money.

» **How did you get started?**

I invested £2500 in some stock, built myself a website and then started marketing! I handed out fliers in my local village and then eventually got some local, national and even international media coverage! It was hard work – integrating the website into card payment systems and working out the customer service systems was tricky. Fortunately, a family friend helped me with the legal aspects of setting up a company, so that wasn't too much of a barrier.

» **What were the biggest challenges that you encountered?**

Selling big shoes, getting returned stock in unusual sizes is tricky as it is difficult to resell these, so you have to write off a lot of stock. Apart from that it's quite difficult being taken seriously by suppliers when you're younger, but then again I got a great amount of media attention, so I suppose that sort of offsets it!

» **What would you say is your greatest accomplishment along on the way?**

How much I learnt. I made an awful amount of mistakes which I have learnt from and this has helped me with other things I have been involved with like university, my current job and GenderChecker.com – my other business. It's also given me the confidence to have a go at running a business again someday.

» **Have you always been interested in this kind of work?**

I was never planning on being a footwear entrepreneur – I just kind of stumbled across it I suppose!

» **What has this experience been like? Any interesting points you would like to share?**

It's been really exciting! I have met some great people, got a feel for how to deal with media attention, and have learnt some fundamental lessons about how to run a business – much better than doing an MBA and reading a whole load of textbooks!

» **What is the most challenging part of your job and why?**

Trying to jump between the high level strategy thinking and the day-to-day customer service is tricky – you tend to get caught up in the moment a bit and don't take enough time to step back and look at the big picture.

» **What fulfillment do you get from your job?**

Helping people find shoes when they really struggled previously is a really pleasing feeling.

» **What important lessons have you learned in the process of establishing your company?**

Don't bet the farm on an untested idea, use your gut feeling to judge things, and build trustworthy relationships with people.

» **What do you think helped you the most in your success?**

My youth – the media attention gave me a fantastic profile and also helped me challenge some conventions and gamble a little! I wouldn't do this again – I'd be reluctant to gamble thousands of pounds, but when I was younger, I didn't fully appreciate the value of money and I suppose in a perverse way, that helped!

» **Where and how do you see yourself five or ten years from now?**

Hopefully running my own business – either in the venture capital industry or some form of technology / online firm – I think these are the areas where there is the most money to be made.

» **What is the most important advice you would give to other entrepreneurs?**

Work hard.

 www.biggerfeet.com

 @oliverbridge

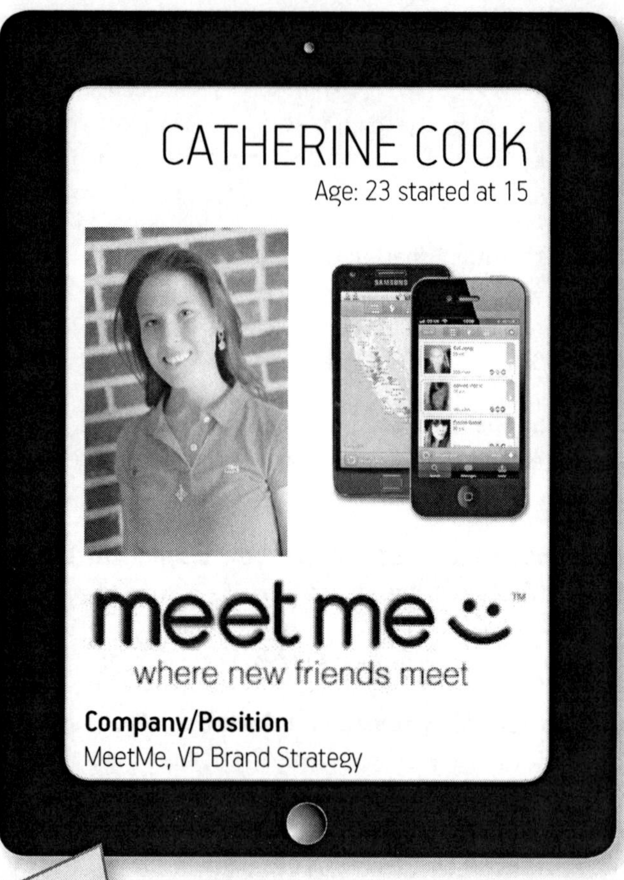

Catherine Cook and her brother created one of the most popular social networking sites in the United States, and were listed as one of the 25 most visited websites in the U.S. MeetMe (formerly MyYearbook) is a social networking service that provides the opportunity to interact and meet new people. MeetMe is the public market leader for social discovery. MeetMe makes meeting people fun through social games and apps, monetized through both advertising and virtual currency. Every day, they help millions of people around the world make new friends whether on the web or their mobile phones.

» **Give a detailed description of the work that you do. What are your job responsibilities?**

I try to make MeetMe the best place to meet new people by conceiving of the next popular features for our mobile apps and site.

» **What made you think of your idea?**

My brother and I got the idea for myYearbook while flipping through a normal high school yearbook back in 2005. We were new in our school, and wanted to make a way to make meeting new friends fun.

» **How did you get started?**

After we got the idea, we found a development team in Mumbai using a site similar to Elance, and sent them hundreds of pages of specifications and pen-on-paper wireframes. We would IM and email them until 3 or 4 in the morning while still having to get up for 7:30am homeroom at our high school. When we launched, we signed up 400 new members the first week and 1 million in the first year, but now we have over 40 million members with 1 million people in the US logging in every day.

» **What were the biggest challenges that you encountered?**

One of the biggest challenges we encountered was how to best change our name. In general people hate it when anything changes about a service they love – just think about Netflix trying to change the DVD service to Qwikster. We worked hard on communicating to the members why we were changing the name to MeetMe, and because of the messaging and all the work our team did, the rebrand was a huge success.

» **What would you say is your greatest accomplishment along on the way?**

My greatest accomplishment is knowing that something we created has helped so many people find good friends. I even met one of my best friends on my own network!

» **How did you get into this job? How easy or difficult it was for you to venture into this business?**

Being an entrepreneur is incredibly risky, and entrepreneurs don't love risk, but we know how to deal with it. When we were first starting out I was in high school so even if the company failed, the worst thing that could happen is I would have to try something new. It wasn't like I needed to pay rent or support a family because I lived at home! Because I was so young, the risk was substantially less, but it took a lot of hard work (and luck) to build myYearbook.

» **Have you always been interested in this kind of work?**

I had wanted to be an entrepreneur since I was 9 or 10 and saw my older brother start a company while he was a student at Harvard. Growing up I knew that I wanted to be an entrepreneur, and that I just needed an idea.

» **What has this experience been like? Any interesting points you would like to share?**

It's been a lot of fun, and definitely very exciting! I love the people I work with; we have an amazing team.

» **What is the most challenging part of your job and why?**

One of the most challenging parts of working on MeetMe is prioritizing what feature to build next. We have a ton of ideas for our site and apps, but we can't build them all at the same time.

» **What fulfillment do you get from your job?**

I love seeing our ideas come to life, and I love hearing our members' stories.

» **What was it like when you realized you made your first million?**

Surreal. I don't really think in those terms; I've always been very down to earth.

» **What important lessons have you learned in the process of establishing your company?**

The most important lessons I've learned are to 1) be about one thing, 2) seek out advice, and 3) don't be afraid to fail. Being about one thing is important because it's impossible to be all things to all people so you have to concentrate on one thing, and then do that one thing very well. Concentrating on only "meeting new people" means that our members will be able to get the most from MeetMe. Seeking out advice is important because you never know absolutely everything you need to know about an idea. It's important to do the research and see what you can learn. Starting out Dave and I didn't really have any knowledge about how to start a company so we had to learn a lot. Luckily, now there are many organizations that help entrepreneurs get started. As Winston Churchill said, "Success is the ability to go from one failure to another with no loss of enthusiasm." As an entrepreneur, you fail a lot. Not every feature launch is a success and not every new product has game changing results, but you need to learn why something may have failed and use it to help you succeed in the future.

» **What do you think helped you the most in your success?**

I think the most important aspect of our success is the team we have at MeetMe. Without them we wouldn't be able to build the features we do. They all come to the office with a passion to make MeetMe the best it possibly can be.

» **Where and how do you see yourself five or ten years from now?**

Five or ten years from now, I see MeetMe as an app everyone has on his or her mobile device and for everyone to know it's the best way to meet new people.

» **How do you spend money – business or personal-wise?**

I spend money very carefully.

» **What is the most important advice you would give to other entrepreneurs?**

I would say the biggest piece of advice is just to go out there and do it. A lot of people can come up with an idea. Ideas are a dime a dozen; it's execution that matters. Aspiring entrepreneurs need to execute quickly and well.

www.meetme.com

@cncook

www.facebook.com/pages/MeetMecom/374599765934434

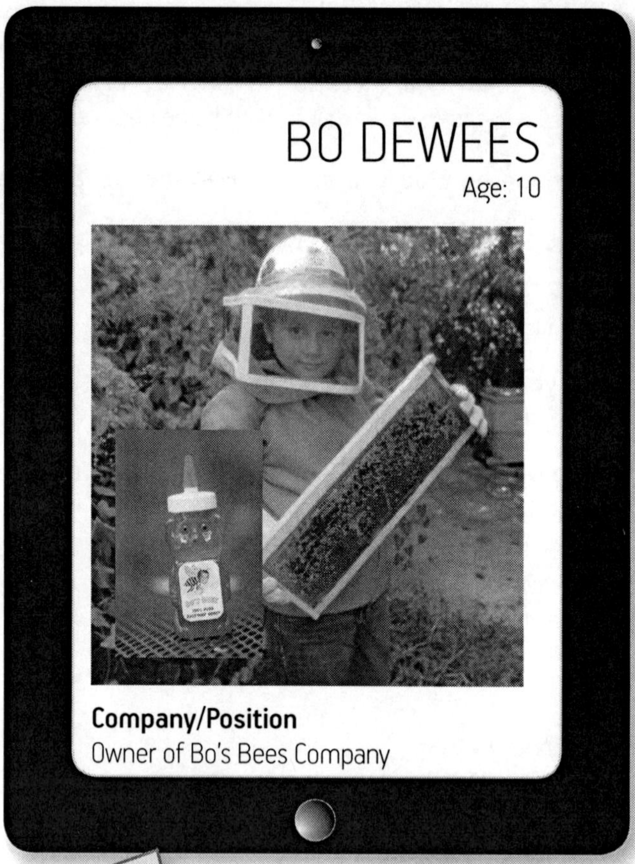

Bo Dewees started making honey in the 3rd grade. Bo's honey is now in high demand, as the makers of Deep Eddy's Sweet Tea Vodka out of Austin Texas now use his honey, you can also find his honey in select stores and online.

» **Give a detailed description of the work that you do. What are your job responsibilities?**

I am Bo's Bee's Head beekeeper. I have to feed the bees with sugar water and then I have to strain the honey, fill the honey bears with honey, clean the jars, dry the jars then label them. I have LOTS of responsibilities!!!The bottles have to be surgically clean and NO moisture or it will turn to sugar and spoil, well it won't spoil but it gets hard.

» **What made you think of your idea?**

My dad helped me because his dad helped him get started. I'm a 3rd generation beekeeper.

» **How did you get started?**

I started with one beehive and have grown it to over 3 million bees.

» **What were the biggest challenges that you encountered?**

Getting stung and the start-up with money.

» **What would you say is your greatest accomplishment along on the way?**

Selling to a major company called Deep Eddy in Austin Texas.

» **How did you get into this job? How easy or difficult it was for you to venture into this business?**

It was pretty easy with some help from my dad.

» **Have you always been interested in this kind of work?**

It's pretty fascinating what a colony of bees can do and how hard they work 24 hours a day 365 days a year.

» **What has this experience been like? Any interesting points you would like to share?**

A bee makes 1/20th of a drop of honey in its lifetime (28 days). 99% of bees are female, which are the only bees with stingers!

» **What is the most challenging part of your job and why?**

Selling it and extracting the honey without getting stung a bunch.

» **What fulfillment do you get from your job?**

I make allot of money and the bees do all the work.

» **What was it like when you realized you made your first million?**

I haven't made a million yet...but I will. I sell out way before I have more to extract and sell. I need more hives then I can really start making millions.

» **What important lessons have you learned in the process of establishing your company?**

Don't let people try and discount your product. The price is the price and it cost a premium because it's the best in town!

» **What do you think helped you the most in your success?**

My dad and grandfather.

» **Where and how do you see yourself five or ten years from now?**

A millionaire with several locations and a good staff of people, like my best friend Richard.

» **How do you spend money – business or personal-wise?**

I invest 95% of my money back into my business and I bought a new baseball glove this year for pitching.

» **What is the most important advice you would give to other entrepreneurs?**

Work hard and spend your money only when necessary. Only accept advice from someone who has done a similar business and has a good reputation. Always stand behind your product and advertise with 10% of your profit when trying to grow. Also be honest with all customers when making change for cash sales.

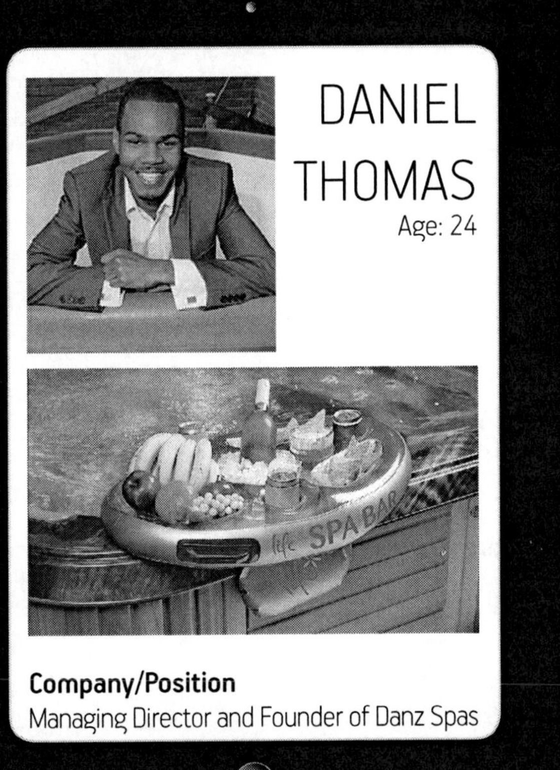

Daniel Thomas began selling items on Ebay while still in college. As his passion for business grew stronger, he wanted to start selling luxury products. Daniel started importing hot tubs at a competitive price from China and started his own company. ***Danz Spas*** are now one of the UK's leading hot tub and spa retailers.

» **Give a detailed description of the work that you do. What are your job responsibilities?**

I'm the founder and owner of Danz Spas. We supply hot tubs throughout the UK and Europe. I'm responsible for the vision and direction of the business.

» **What made you think of your idea?**

We started off selling a wide range of products on eBay whilst I was in college (what you would call high school in the states). Everything started to go downhill and our sales decreased massively. I then decided to focus on one product and build a 'real' business out of it. I chose hot tubs because it meant we only needed a small range (a big one, a small one, and one in the middle!) and wouldn't have to hold huge amounts of stock.

» **How did you get started?**

I found a supplier in China, made a website, and started advertising on google.

» **What were the biggest challenges that you encountered?**

Money: hot tubs are expensive items. It's difficult to find the cash up front to order them in.

» **What would you say is your greatest accomplishment along on the way?**

We've now sold over 1000 hot tubs throughout Europe and have provided hot tubs to a number of UK celebrities.

» **Have you always been interested in this kind of work?**

I can't say I've always been interested in hot tubs but I have certainly always wanted to run my own business.

» **What has this experience been like? Any interesting points you would like to share?**

Very challenging, but very rewarding.

» **What is the most challenging part of your job and why?**

I'm a very young an inexperience manager so management isn't particularly my forte.

» **What fulfillment do you get from your job?**

I get to see something which I have created grow. We provide

» **What important lessons have you learned in the process of establishing your company?**

Take things slow, don't rush. Don't assume you are always right. Mistakes are a blessing if you learn from them.

» **What do you think helped you the most in your success?**
Perseverance.

» **Where and how do you see yourself five or ten years from now?**
Hopefully Married with a few kids enjoying the success of my business!

» **How do you spend money – business or personal-wise?**
I try to be prudent. We keep a very close eye on the company accounts.

» **What is the most important advice you would give to other entrepreneurs?**
Make sure you are doing something you enjoy and learn from your mistakes.

 www.danz.co.uk

 @danzspas

 www.facebook.com/danzspas

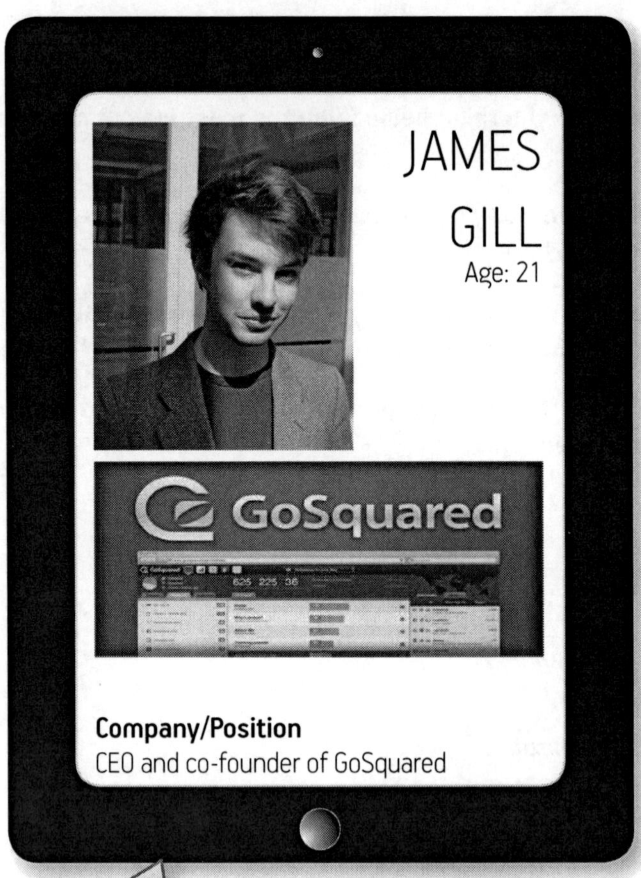

James Gill is an intelligent young entrepreneur from Britain. His company has become so successful they even had a visit from UK Prime Minister David Cameron. GoSquared helps you understand and improve your online presence. GoSquared creates two web applications for monitoring your website's traffic. Real-time analytics for your website. GoSquared helps you monitor, understand and improve your websites.

» Give a detailed description of the work that you do. What are your job responsibilities?

I'm the CEO and co-founder of GoSquared – I spend my day managing our team of 8 people, planning where we go next, talking to customers to understand what we can do better, and meeting people to push us forward.

» What made you think of your idea?

We started working on GoSquared while still at school. We originally built GoSquared as an advertising platform, and found there to be more opportunity for us to innovate in the analytics space. At the time, most analytics services gave you data that was hours, if not days old. GoSquared has always given you up to the second, real-time data.

» How did you get started?

I built a blog a long time ago and have always loved design and drawing. I've always been a creative individual. I had an idea and then I found two amazing cofounders to work on it with me – Geoff and JT.

» What were the biggest challenges that you encountered?

Getting people to notice us. We spent months, if not years, trying to get our voices heard. The best thing we ever did was start a blog to talk about what we are working on and share our story. You'd be amazed at how much you can help people just by sharing what you're doing.

» What would you say is your greatest accomplishment along on the way?

Building a passionate, incredibly talented team that loves what they're doing.

» How did you get into this job? How easy or difficult it was for you to venture into this business?

I started this while at school. We took a gap year after school to work on GoSquared full-time. Geoff and I got our places sorted for uni after the gap year, but were approached by investors in London one week before going. Then we went to uni for 5 weeks before dropping out and starting up in London.

» Have you always been interested in this kind of work?

I've always wanted to run my own company and I've always wanted to be closely involved in the design and creation of a product used by thousands of people, so I guess so.

» **What has this experience been like? Any interesting points you would like to share?**

I always underestimated how hard it would be grow a team. When you're 3 people you know what each other are doing and you spend next to no time having meetings or catch up sessions because everything is autonomous. When you scale that up, even to 5 people, you start having to communicate in a whole different manner. It's something we've had to learn on the go. Also, you're nothing without customers – treat them how you'd love to be treated.

» **What is the most challenging part of your job and why?**

Going to sleep – I have no time for it, and I never like to waste a minute that I know I can be spending taking GoSquared to the next level.

» **What fulfillment do you get from your job?**

It's the most fulfilling thing I could be doing with my life right now – building a product that's used by thousands of customers around the world, from individuals up to large corporations, is a huge responsibility. There's nothing better than hearing from a happy customer who tells you you've made their day better.

» **What do you think helped you the most in your success?**

I didn't go to a University – that may have been stupid, but if I had gone after our gap year everything we had worked on to that point would have gone to waste. By sticking at it, and taking a route that not many people want to, it seems we've been able to achieve a lot in a short space of time.

» **Where and how do you see yourself five or ten years from now?**

We shall see where technology takes us. I want to run my own businesses, and they will always be very focused on solving real problems, have the highest appreciation of good design, and show an unparalleled care for customer service. If I'm honest, I can't tell you where I'll be one year from now.

» **How do you spend money – business or personal-wise?**

Starting this year, I'm trying to obey a stricter policy of saving a proportion of everything I earn. Last year I spent more than I should – I enjoy treating others and I enjoy treating myself. I'm going to try scaling that back a bit.

» **What is the most important advice you would give to other entrepreneurs?**

Don't give up too soon. Start small, iterate quickly, and get honest feedback from smart people who aren't afraid to tell you when you've made a mistake.

www.gosquared.com

@jamesjgill

www.facebook.com/GoSquared

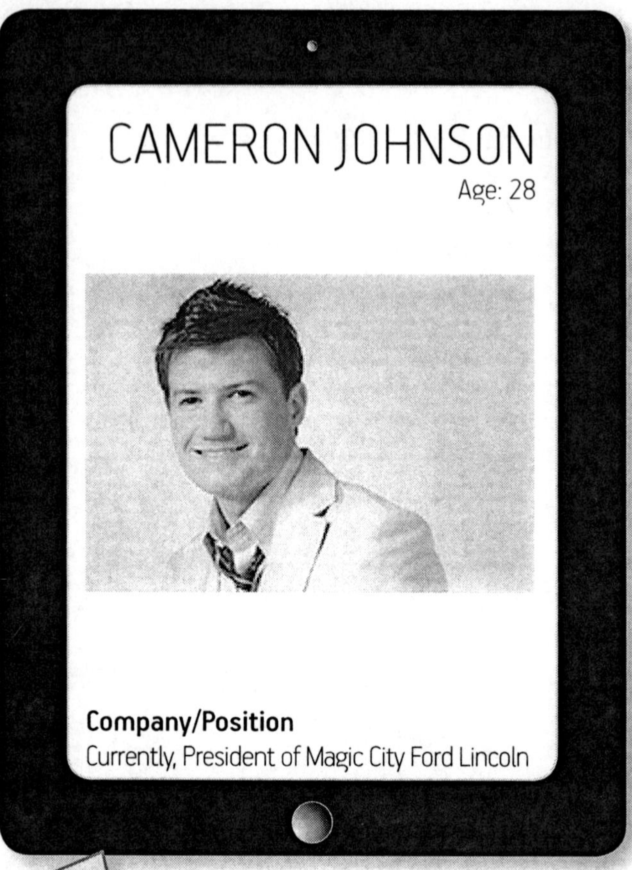

Cameron started his first business at the age of nine and before graduating high school he was recognized as one of the most successful young entrepreneurs in the world. As a teenager he started a dozen profitable businesses and at 15, he became the youngest American appointed to the board of a Tokyo-based company. Last year, Cameron was a finalist on Oprah Winfrey's first prime time series, The Big Give, which aired on ABC. Most recently, he hosted Season 4 of Beat the Boss which airs on the BBC in the UK.

» **Give a detailed description of the work that you do. What are your job responsibilities?**

So I'm currently the President & CEO of Magic City Ford Lincoln, a family owned car dealership in Virginia. Previously, I started 12 internet companies while I was growing up – beginning when I was 9 years old.

» **What made you think of your idea?**

I started my first business after getting a computer and printer as a Christmas present from my parents and was making $50k/year by the age of 12.

» **What were the biggest challenges that you encountered?**

I'd first say my age proved to be both a challenge as well as an advantage. Without the internet, I would have never been able to start my businesses and would have been limited to just a lemonade stand, etc. The Internet enabled me to reach a global marketplace and it didn't matter my age. My age helped generate endless media attention which was essentially free advertising for my various companies. At the same time, I'd hide my age when I thought it would hurt me when dealing with people who might have been much older. So sometimes it could hurt but more often, it definitely helped.

» **What would you say is your greatest accomplishment along on the way?**

Each accomplishment/milestone was the best until I reached the next goal. I was always goal driven. My company had 200,000 customers when I was 15 and I was the Youngest American to join the Board of a Japanese based company when I was 15. I also wrote a bestselling book in Japan when I was 15 and had a bestselling book in the US when I was 21. When I was 25, I was named one of the Ten Outstanding Young Americans – which was definitely a highlight.

» **How did you get into this job? How easy or difficult it was for you to venture into this business?**

I always started my own businesses by starting with an idea.

» **Have you always been interested in this kind of work?**

All of my businesses were different and I had 12 over 12 years – all of which were profitable – so I'd often get interested in an idea/opportunity and start that business, grow it/sell it and move to the next idea. My "favorite" idea was always the one that I was about to start next.

» **What has this experience been like? Any interesting points you would like to share?**

My book You Call the Shots – Succeed Your Way and Live the Life You Want with the 19 Essential Secrets of Entrepreneurship – really outlines my story but a few tidbits: Put Yourself Out There, Start Small, Adapt or Die, and Be the Entrepreneur You Want to Be.

» **What is the most challenging part of your job and why?**
The time commitment and dedication.

» **What fulfillment do you get from your job?**
The reward when starting/launching a business and the satisfaction when making deals/growing.

» **What was it like when you realized you made your first million?**
It has a nice ring to it but having $999k or $1.01k isn't all that different. You are still an entrepreneur and it was never about the money.

» **What do you think helped you the most in your success?**
Not knowing what I can't do – I always had the attitude "why not me?"

» **Where and how do you see yourself five or ten years from now?**
Still starting businesses, running my Ford Dealership, perhaps buying other businesses, etc.

» **How do you spend money – business or personal-wise?**
Investments and Travel.

» **What is the most important advice you would give to other entrepreneurs?**
Put yourself out there. Doesn't matter if you're the smartest guy/girl in the world or if you have a cure for a disease or a product that people must have – if you don't put yourself out there, nothing will happen.

 www.cameronjohnson.com

 @cameronjohnson

 www.facebook.com/cameronjohnson

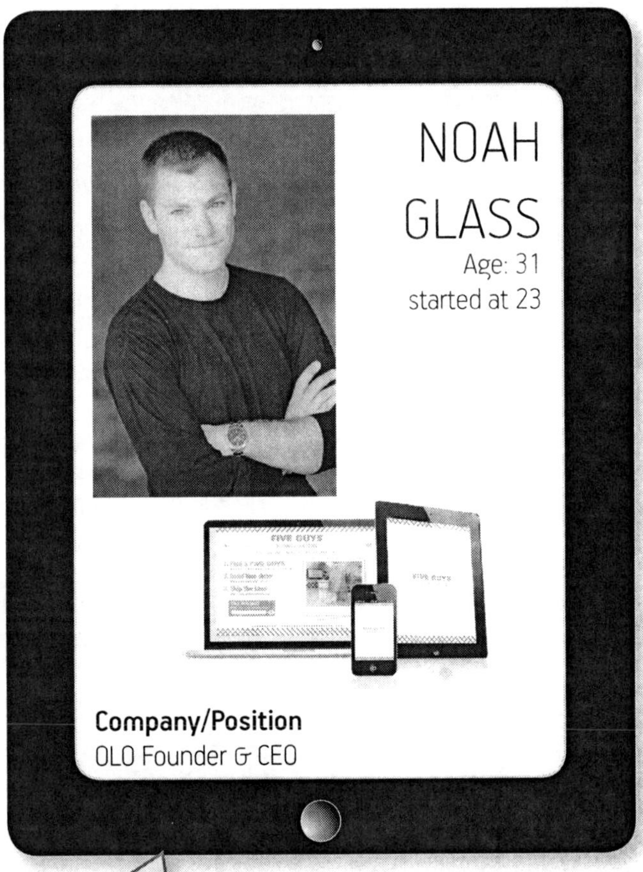

Noah began working in the foodservice industry as a cashier, server, bartender, and delivery driver before founding OLO. Noah graduated from Yale University with a degree in Political Science and is well-known for having withdrawn his admission to Harvard Business School to start OLO. ***OLO*** is now the original and best-in-class online and mobile ordering provider for restaurants. OLO is the fastest-growing self-service ordering provider for the foodservice industry.

» **Give a detailed description of the work that you do. What are your job responsibilities?**

I lead the OLO management team in maintaining the best-in-class digital commerce engine for the restaurant industry, allowing customers to order and pay from their smart phones and "Skip the Line(r)" at busy restaurants.

» **What made you think of your idea?**

Waiting in long lines for coffee and lunch at restaurants here in New York City. And seeing the rise of smart phones coming during my time living abroad in 2004.

» **How did you get started?**

Built a MVP (minimum viable product) prototype with two web developers. Showed it to a couple of investors. One offered to provide us with $500k in seed capital if I quit my job and withdrew my early admission to Harvard Business School. I said "yes" to that offer immediately. OLO was on its way.

» **What were the biggest challenges that you encountered?**

Launching in 2005 with a mobile ordering service meant that we were "too early." Remember that iPhone did not hit until late 2007. We had to spend many years educating the market (restaurants and customers) about why ordering and paying ahead was a good thing.

» **What would you say is your greatest accomplishment along on the way?**

Keeping our eyes on the prize, never giving up, and persevering through many challenges. A startup achieving profitability after seven years of struggle is a rare thing.

» **Have you always been interested in this kind of work?**

Always. And especially after working at Shutterfly.com as an intern in Summer 2000 (the height of the .com boom) and working at Endeavor.org, where I was exposed to incredible entrepreneurs in emerging market countries around the world.

» **What has this experience been like? Any interesting points you would like to share?**

Incredibly challenging and gratifying. I never knew how difficult things could get and how resilient the team and I would have to be. The saying "it's always darkest before the dawn" has rung true many, many times.

» **What is the most challenging part of your job and why?**

Firing people is the hardest thing and always will be. Especially in such a small company. It's very, very emotional.

» **What fulfillment do you get from your job?**

I am incredibly honored to work with a team that inspires me on a daily basis. Our engineering team and our client services team are second to none. It's a thrill.

» **What was it like when you realized you made your first million?**

When the company first booked over $1M in revenue, I realized that we had achieved a major milestone. Even more significant was achieving profitability. That felt incredible and we celebrated heartily.

» **What important lessons have you learned in the process of establishing your company?**

Perseverance is everything.

» **What do you think helped you the most in your success?**

The sheer will to win and to do the best for my employees and investors.

» **Where and how do you see yourself five or ten years from now?**

I hope I'm still running OLO and helping to realize its full potential.

» **How do you spend money – business or personal-wise?**

I spend free time and money making memories with my wife and family and being good to the people I love in one way or another.

» **What is the most important advice you would give to other entrepreneurs?**

Have the courage to get started. Have the fortitude to keep going.

 www.olo.com

 @nhglass

 www.facebook.com/olodotcom

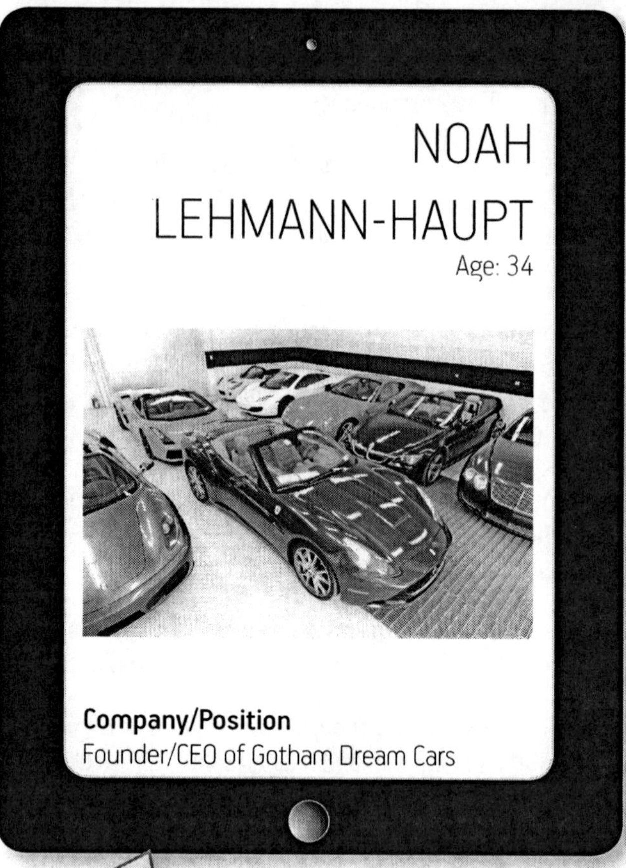

Noah Lehmann-Haupt bought his first Ferrari when he was just 25. He began renting it out and used the profits to buy another luxury car. Noah's passion grew and Gotham Dream Cars was created. Gotham Dream Cars specializes in exotic rentals including Ferrari, Lamborghini and luxury sports ***cars***. Gotham Dream Cars provides membership information, pricing and reservations.

» **Give a detailed description of the work that you do. What are your job responsibilities?**

Overall vision and "big boss stuff" for the company. My COO runs day-to-day operations so my main role these days is to make sure we make good strategic decisions (i.e. we're heading in the right direction) and that the warehouse doesn't burn down.

» **What made you think of your idea?**

I wanted to rent a fun car back in 2003 to do a cross-country drive and couldn't find a place to do it. So I made my own.

» **How did you get started?**

Lots of phone calls to insurance companies, lots of research, and lots of time planning and reading.

» **What were the biggest challenges that you encountered?**

Took over 9 months to find an insurance company willing to provide coverage to a one-man operation with a single Ferrari in New York City.

» **What would you say is your greatest accomplishment along on the way?**

This picture:

Senator Edward Kennedy,Washington, D.C.

Aston Martin Vanquish. Fulfilling a lifelong dream of her husband's, thoughtful Mrs. Victoria Kennedy rented our Aston Martin Vanquish as a birthday-weekend gift for a surprised (and excited!) Senator Edward Kennedy.

» **How did you get into this job? How easy or difficult it was for you to venture into this business?**
Not easy, but fun.

» **Have you always been interested in this kind of work?**
I've always been interested in being my own boss -- I love building things (companies, products, etc.

» **What has this experience been like? Any interesting points you would like to share?**
Wonderful - I've learned a lot about managing a team of people, about what work I like (and what I dislike) and what sort of stuff I want to do in the future.

» **What is the most challenging part of your job and why?**
The unexpected -- everyone likes stability and comfort, even bosses. Getting the 2am phone calls that a car broke down the night before a big wedding rental is a pain sometimes.

» **What fulfillment do you get from your job?**
I love being my own boss. Love being able to set my own schedule every day. Love being able to build something and see it take shape.

» **What important lessons have you learned in the process of establishing your company?**
The single most important lesson I learned is that many companies ignore the little things (like hiring a bookkeeper) and that is one of the most incredibly important things you can do as early as possible.

» **What do you think helped you the most in your success?**
Having a good network of friends and advisors who know way more than I do about this sort of stuff.

» **Where and how do you see yourself five or ten years from now?**
I hope, building more businesses and products!

» **How do you spend money – business or personal-wise?**
Wisely and carefully.

» **What is the most important advice you would give to other entrepreneurs?**
Don't be discouraged by people who question your decision to be an entrepreneur - most people are petrified at the thought of striking out on their

own and jealous that you've made the decision to do it, so will respond by trying to drag you down. BUT - don't think that all advice is negative advice - listen to smart people who have genuine criticisms of your idea. Being able to differentiate between good feedback (positive or negative) and "haters" is very very important.

www.gothamdreamcars.com

@noahlh

www.facebook.com/gothamdreamcars

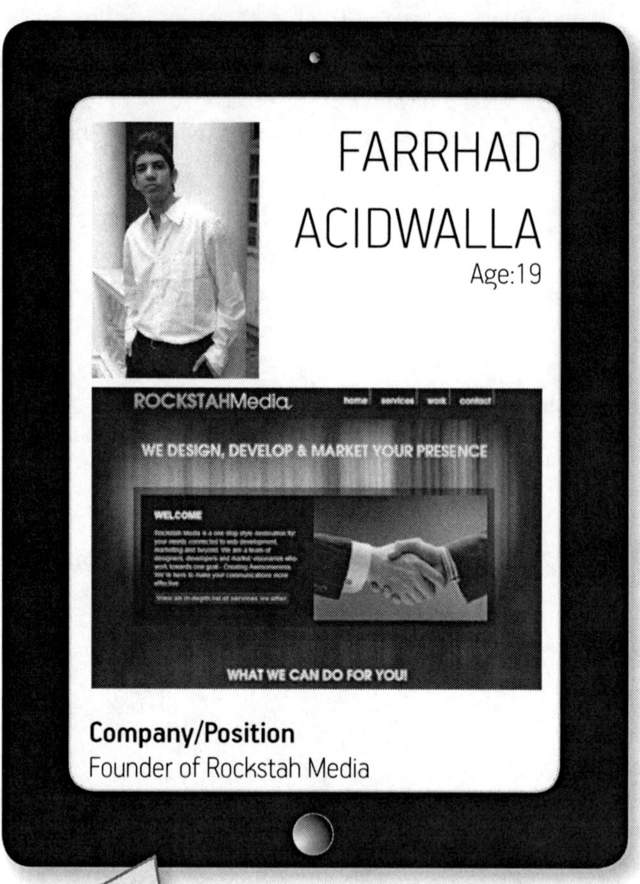

Farrhad Acidwalla is from Mumbai, Maharashtra, India. At the age of 12, he started an aviation website which was a successful community. He then went on to venture in more projects. Then in 2009 he founded a company called Rockstah Media. Rockstah Media, is an award winning team that specializes in Web Development, Marketing, Branding, Events and Celebrity Management.

» **Give a detailed description of the work that you do. What are your job responsibilities?**

Current job responsibilities include day to day communication with clients and understanding what they need and how they want their work done. I also play a small role in the initial design process but the design team mainly takes that forward.

» **What made you think of your idea?**

I started off with an aviation website and ended up selling it for a sum far higher than what I'd invested in it. This process repeated itself with some other projects too and I figured I was doing something right.

» **How did you get started?**

I didn't start off with the intention of forming a company, but a chain of events just led to it.

» **What were the biggest challenges that you encountered?**

Age was a factor earlier. But now that there's a lot of work to our credit and the hard work is paying off- it is easier to get clients now than it was earlier when I was younger.

» **What would you say is your greatest accomplishment along on the way?**

There's still a lot more to do. I'm still just 19 but I'm really happy that I've formed a great team and we're able to deliver better results than our client's expect. So that does feel quite good!

» **Have you always been interested in this kind of work?**

I had no clue that this was my field! Was a chain of events that just led to it. Taking that one first step is always the most important.

» **What important lessons have you learned in the process of establishing your company?**

A journey of a thousand miles begins with one step. Taking that first step is always the most important. If I hadn't taken that one step I wouldn't be here today. Also, trust your instincts and move ahead and try being the best version of yourself you can.

» **What do you think helped you the most in your success?**

Never, never, never give up. And my parents have been really supportive too and have always been there to advise me when I needed it.

» **Where and how do you see yourself five or ten years from now?**

I haven't actually thought that ahead to be honest! I take each day as it comes. I've founded two new companies recently. For now, I'm concentrating on taking them to the next level.

» **How do you spend money – business or personal-wise?**

Personal: A little bit on gaming and a little bit on partying! Not too much though.

» **What is the most important advice you would give to other entrepreneurs?**

Failure is the stepping stone to success. There is no changing that- Try, try until you succeed. Do not give up easily, always push forward. Also, money isn't everything. There's a lot more to life than that.

 www.rockstahmedia.com

 @Farrhad

 www.facebook.com/RockstahMedia

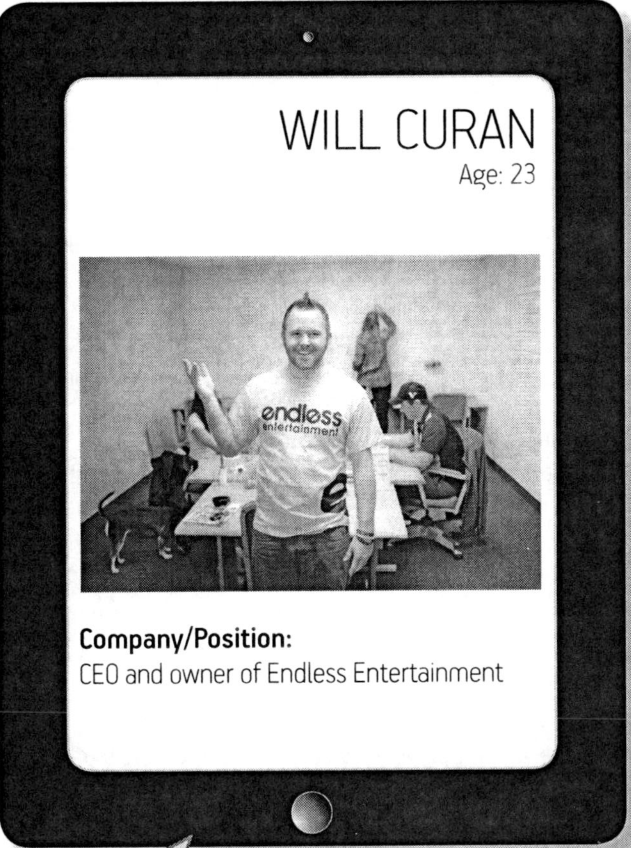

WILL CURAN

Age: 23

Company/Position:
CEO and owner of Endless Entertainment

Will turned his passions for music and entertainment into a million dollar industry. Endless Entertainment is your ultimate entertainment source. They do everything from DJs, MCs, Live Percussionists, and Dance crews, visual productions, enhancing event atmosphere, building experiences around brands, and much more.

» **Give a detailed description of the work that you do. What are your job responsibilities?**

My job responsibilities are constantly shifting, as the owner and president of the company, I have been known to do a little bit of everything. I really believe in working on your business rather than working in it. I have been a huge advocate of working on your business, so I spend a lot of time working on sales, managing my staff, working on marketing campaigns, working on the finances of the company, human resources, I have been known to defiantly do a little bit of everything, but the big thing with me is I am the owner of the company so I have to lead my team to do their job and make sure we are all going along with the same vision and getting the jobs that they need to be doing done.

» **What made you think of your idea?**

It all started back in high school, when I was a freshman and I had an internet radio station I started literally out of my bedroom, and I grew it and grew it, and gained more and more listeners, actually grew to 125 listeners at anytime, which is a lot for an internet radio station. The problem was that back in the day it cost me about 400$ a month to run, which 400$ when you are a freshman in high school is a lot, it still is a lot of money, that's a car payment right there. So I ended up shutting it down because it was costing me to much money to run. Everyone was telling me at the time hey you should try Djing, so from there I bought myself a little dj in a box kit, literally djing in my bedroom just for fun, that's literally all I did. And I have always had a huge love for music, still love music today; I am listening to music all the time. There's hardly ever a time I am not listening to music. So I kept djing and I loved it, and I had never djed for anyone before except for online with my internet radio station. Someone actually told me you should dj at my backyard party and I didn't really know hip hop, all I knew was electronic music, which is popular now but wasn't then, and I was like you know what Il do it, and she paid me 50$ to do it, and I felt like I was the richest guy in the world. I had a blast doing it even though I didn't really know what I was doing at first. So I started doing my own high school dances, and from there all the middle schools around Arizona and it just kept growing and growing and I kept doing more and more gigs. I didn't know anything about business or marketing, I started Djing all over the place. From there I came to ACU, and I came here on a full ride entrepreneurship scholarship for starting a business I had no idea what I was doing, from there I got a grant from the university for 20,000$ and an office space, and that's what really turned it into a real company. It then became how do we hire people to do this, how do we make more money, and it kind of just grew from there, and we just did bigger and bigger shows, and then we started getting bigger events like x games, and all of these huge events, and then back in July we were branded into MS entertainment because we wanted to be something for then a Dj company we wanted to be this mass entertainment brand. So we named it MS entertainment and it's kind of been history ever since. The whole reason this kind of came up was I had crappy high school dances, I don't know about you but my high school dances sucked, I was always trying to improve that experience. So that is why I originally started was to make high school dances better.

» **What were the biggest challenges that you encountered?**

I was defiantly not lacking on the challenge side of things. I still have challenges every day. My big thing is I never have to learn twice. If something happens, I am never going to let that happen again. An example of when I first started I knew how to dj but I didn't know how to do hip hop or top 40 or anything like that, so I had to learn the music and from there I had to learn how to entertain people and how do I make it a really great event. What happens when a speaker goes on at an event? How do you make people happy? I learned from the ground up how to entertain people. From there it got a lot harder, because entertaining people is actually pretty easy. The hard part is dealing with the company, learning how to hire people, not to hire friends, not to hire family, and focusing on hiring people that are going to bring your vision to life. That is one of the challenges I constantly ran into. Other things are I am really young so I don't have a lot of credit history and the economy being the way it is, I couldn't walk into a bank and ask for a loan, just getting the money you need to grow, growing this company without any outside investments was a challenge. Age was also a challenge, because when you are really young it's easy for people to not take credit for what you can do, so we are constantly fighting the age barrier.

» **What would you say is your greatest accomplishment along on the way?**

I kind of take it in steps. I don't like to say there is one defining moment. I try to celebrate the wins as much as I can. I celebrate with my team, I celebrate with everyone. We have done so many great events, anything from target to Tostitos fiesta bowl, to the x games; we have a lot of really great clients. I have been really grateful for all of the accomplishments I have done. My ability to work really hard and not burn out, I have been really thankful for that. My job requires me to sometimes work till 3 or 4 am, and then be in the office at 8am the next day, so I think being able to work hard is a great accomplishment, and it's something I have been really really grateful I can do.

» **What has this experience been like? Any interesting points you would like to share?**

I find my job fascinating and I love doing it, it's hard for me to say one thing without going on for years.

» **What important lessons have you learned in the process of establishing your company?**

Personal life balance is something. One of the big things is for people to realize that entrepreneurship is not just about creation. Everyone likes to say to be an entrepreneur you have to create the next facebook or twitter, or the next drug that's going to cure millions of people, or this next device that's going to enhance the human race. People need to realize it's about building a business, building something that you love, not just something new, there are millions of businesses out there that have done the same things as millions of other companies, there's millions of pizza shops out there. My idea was nothing new, there has been a company doing this since I have been alive. The big thing that I came in to do was figure out a way to enhance it, change it, doing it better. That's where you are going to be really successful, and ultimately be happy, if you are doing what you love, it doesn't have to be a new idea. I think a lot of people think that they have to create this amazing new product but no you don't have to, do something that you love, and do something you would love to make money doing.

» **What do you think helped you the most in your success?**

I think that school is great for some people. I was really lucky my school has a lot of really amazing resources for entrepreneurs that kind of helped kick start me and get me in the right direction but honestly anyone that ever says school, or some resource is the reason why they became successful, the true reason you really became successful was because they used that resource and their own personal drive and work ambition utilized that resource because it's all going to come within you. One of the reasons I am so successful is because I have a huge appetite for improving and making things better. I am not one to give up very easily. The second a problem pops up, I am researching it, I am trying figure out how I can fix it. I'm doing a million things at once, to make it so that I can improve, and grow the company.

» **Where and how do you see yourself five or ten years from now?**

Woo, 5 years were hoping to be 5 million in revenue, we want to be coast to coast, 10 years now, I don't usually think that far ahead because things change so much, but 10 years...double quadruple, stand out even more, I would love to start doing stuff globally, bigger and bigger events. We are currently building our brand.

» **What is the most important advice you would give to other entrepreneurs?**

I always try to tell something different every time I am interviewed, because there is so much that can help somebody. One of the most recent things

I have been able to get is that when you are a young entrepreneur your personal life and your business life are stressful. It's easy to get stressed out, I will literally be working for days straight working in the office Monday through Friday, for example this weekend tomorrow I will driving to a speaking engagement, then Sunday I have a show, Monday and Tuesday I will be in the office, Wednesday I have a show, Thursday I will be in the office, Friday I will be in the office, Saturday I have a show, so it is literally days upon days of work. It's just so easy to get burnt out, and especially in your personal life, personal relationships. Being able to realize you are very hyper career focused when you're young is OK. For me I don't get to go out much because I am working on the weekends. For you to be able to understand that your personal relationships are going to be sacrificed but that's ok and that you can figure out ways to still hang out with your friends still take breaks and still have fun you will be able to be very successful, because you will be able to manage your stress load and stay happy at the same time. You shouldn't do something that doesn't make you happy; the second you are questioning should I be doing this you should start doing something else.

www.helloendless.com

@djWillSee

www.facebook.com/helloendless

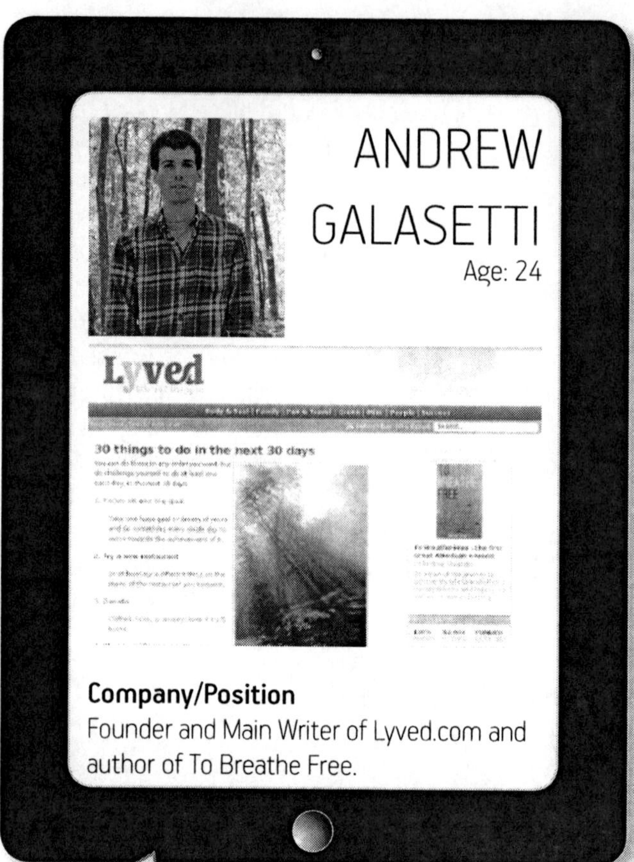

Andrew is an artist, entrepreneur, and author who has brought his ideas to life at a young age. Lyved is a blogzine (mix between blog and magazine articles) that focuses on various aspects of life; from business to news, to the environment and personal growth; and even some politics once and awhile. Lyved provides quality content that prides itself on having a fresh and positive perspective on life and living it.

» **Give a detailed description of the work that you do. What are your job responsibilities?**

My responsibilities are varied. For Lyved.com, I write content, promote on social media sites, coordinate guest posts, and maintain the backend of the website. For To Breathe Free, a novel I am working on, I write and edit my manuscript, as well as promote on social media sites and continue to pitch media outlets.

» **What made you think of your idea?**

Prior to Lyved and To Breathe Free, I had countless ideas which I pursued; however, I never took my innate talent for writing seriously until I was encouraged by high school teachers. Soon after graduating, I launched Lyved in college so that I could write to empower readers.

» **How did you get started?**

To launch both Lyved and my novel, I did research first and learned as much as I could about what I was getting into. For instance, for Lyved, I learned about blogging systems like WordPress and learned how to set up a professional website Then like all entrepreneurs should do, I dove in. You eventually have to dive in and learn from experience and your mistakes.

» **What were the biggest challenges that you encountered?**

Getting my writing out to readers. With millions of blogs and millions of books in the world, you need to be noticed by being different.

» **What would you say is your greatest accomplishment along on the way?**

Lyved and To Breathe Free have been mentioned on very popular websites and in other media outlets which always feels like a great accomplishment. But what is the greatest feeling to me is when a reader contacts me and expresses how much they have been impacted by my writing and what I'm doing. It's an amazing experience that can't be replicated.

» **How did you get into this job? How easy or difficult it was for you to venture into this business?**

I came to writing naturally. Creativity and the arts is something that is in my family genes. Every venture is difficult and should be. You can't succeed without challenges.

» **Have you always been interested in this kind of work?**

Just about. I have always been interested in the arts and writing. And from the age of fourteen, I have pursued entrepreneurialism.

- **What has this experience been like? Any interesting points you would like to share?**

It's always challenging but also always interesting. No day is ever the same and that is one of the things I enjoy so much about entrepreneurialism and writing.

- **What is the most challenging part of your job and why?**

I think juggling so many roles at once is probably the most difficult part. There are only so many hours in a day and it's important to stop and enjoy life as well.

- **What fulfillment do you get from your job?**

The fulfillment I get from my job is the same as I stated in question 5: knowing that my writing and what I'm doing is positively impacting people.

- **What was it like when you realized you made your first million?**

I have not made my first million. When I started as an entrepreneur, millions of dollars was my main focus. As I grew, I shifted my focus. I certainly want to be comfortable and not have to worry about bills but I pursue different goals like impacting people, which is much more fulfilling than earning money. It touches your soul. Something money cannot do.

- **What important lessons have you learned in the process of establishing your company?**

Probably more lessons that I could ever express in one sitting but I think one of the important lessons comes from my response in number 11. Don't follow the "Almighty Dollar."

- **What do you think helped you the most in your success?**

My failures. I've learned so much from them that I couldn't learn anywhere else.

- **Where and how do you see yourself five or ten years from now?**

I would love to continue to be an entrepreneur, writer, and explore any endeavor that is challenging and creative.

- **How do you spend money – business or personal-wise?**

At the moment I'm quite frugal. So whenever I make a purchase, even if it is for some personal enjoyment, I try to find ways that my entrepreneurial pursuits will benefit as well. So reinvesting is probably how I spend most of my money.

» **What is the most important advice you would give to other entrepreneurs?**

The same advice as I mentioned above. Don't pursue the goal of making millions. Focus on your passion and helping others.

www.andrewgalasetti.com

@AndrewGalasetti

www.facebook.com/andrewgalasetti

JACOB KENT-LEDGER

Age: 18

kentledger

Company/Position
Founder/Owner/Creative Director – KentLedger Media

Jacob is an 18 Year old passion driven entrepreneur with many achievements and successes at a young age. This entrepreneur is from the U.K. and started up a successful company while still in school. Kentledger Media is a creative branding agency with a vast experience in commercial marketing, branding and specializing in logos, advertising and website design.

» Give a detailed description of the work that you do. What are your job responsibilities?

I work with a large clientele on a daily basis, negotiating projects, delegating roles out to my team of staff and consulting businesses on how to improve their image. My responsibilities are to manage the company, staff and incoming work to ensure it is all to a high standard that the company so famously promotes and that all clients are entirely satisfied with their work. I am also a public speaker so some days are spent attending events to talk about business and enterprise to young people.

» What made you think of your idea?

I realized there were a lot of similar businesses as it's a very crowded market but I had the experience and wanted to try it out as a business. I was racking my brain every night for a long time to think up an invention but in the end, I realized a profit making idea was right in front of me and KentLedger was born. Despite there being a lot of competition, I have managed to outmaneuver other companies who now adopt similar price structures as us as we can offer a more affordable service to our clients.

» How did you get started?

I set up a website for the company and told a few people about it, then I started looking for work and an office company needed some designs so that was the first bit of work. It came in within the first week of officially trading and led to many other clients over the coming months.

» What were the biggest challenges that you encountered?

The biggest challenge to date would be time management. I decided to set up my business just after starting a year of exams so it wasn't brilliant timing but I'm now supported by my excellent team of staff and sales manager Sam. It is an indescribable feeling when you overcome a challenge in business.

» What would you say is your greatest accomplishment along on the way?

I believe my greatest accomplishment would be working with a company very early on and then getting an email later on to be told the work designed for them would be at every fuel station across the United Kingdom. It blew me away and is still a very vocal point in what I consider achievements in business.

» How did you get into this job? How easy or difficult it was for you to venture into this business?

I had a lot of commercial experience in retail, Film & TV, security and media so decided to enter the creative scene as a bit of a game. The way I saw it, I had no startup costs so I had nothing to lose. I wanted to see where it would take me and I've never looked back.

» **Have you always been interested in this kind of work?**

From an early age, I never really had any inkling as to what job or career was for me but once I established my business, I realized just how interested I was in the sector and that turning my passion into my business was an excellent move which I don't regret.

» **What has this experience been like? Any interesting points you would like to share?**

It's been a journey more than anything. I started with one small dream and have come so far. Meeting celebrities, business figures and inspiring people along the way has been an incredible and amazing set of experiences. My favorite experience would be meeting Sir Richard Branson after being invited to speak to him one-to-one at an event. It was so surreal and a pleasant experience to meet someone so passionate about business and success.

» **What is the most challenging part of your job and why?**

I face many challenges on a daily basis. I'd say the biggest part is having a social life! I want this business to work and it means putting endless hours and hard graft in to get the results I want to achieve. It's just a bit of a sacrifice for a few years while I concentrate on growing the business.

» **What fulfillment do you get from your job?**

The fulfillment from my job is off the scale. I would honestly not swap it for anything. The saying 'be your own boss' is so underrated and you won't know until you try it.

» **What important lessons have you learned in the process of establishing your company?**

Don't rush anything when getting into business. It's easy just to think up a name and start selling your product or service. There's a lot more involved, mainly legal work. Terms and conditions are key and copyrights or trademarks if necessary. It's easy to get caught out if you haven't covered every angle.

» **What do you think helped you the most in your success?**

The people around me. I've tried to surround myself with similar like-minded people to ensure I think positively and actively about business and can come to them for any support or advice. I have a huge network of entrepreneurs and business owners who can help in a second. A strong network is a great way to get your business out there too.

» **Where and how do you see yourself five or ten years from now?**

Ideally, on a beach in southern France. Well we can all dream right? No, seriously, we should all have dreams. Nothing's impossible, I mean the words 'I'm possible' are even spelt out in it! I'd like to become an international business as well as public speaker for larger corporate events, supporting charities and youth organizations. We can't predict the future but hard work will always see a good return in my eyes.

» **How do you spend money – business or personal-wise?**

Business money is reinvested to improve the brand where possible and resources available to staff. It's all part of becoming an eco-sustainable enterprise too as we're pledging to be an environmentally friendly company. Personal money just goes on the normal necessities of life; car, fuel, food!

» **What is the most important advice you would give to other entrepreneurs?**

An economic downturn is the best time to set up a business. No really it is so listen up! People are in a receptive state during any downturn and your idea could very well strike a win with them if you tap into the economy and exploit legitimately an opportunity to grow a business. This has been seen with recycling firms, payday lenders and startup support agencies. Work hard every day because time is so precious and will be so worth it. Spend a few years of your life how others don't, so that you can spend the rest of your life how others can't.

 www.kentledger.com

 @JacobKentLedger

 www.facebook.com/KentLedger

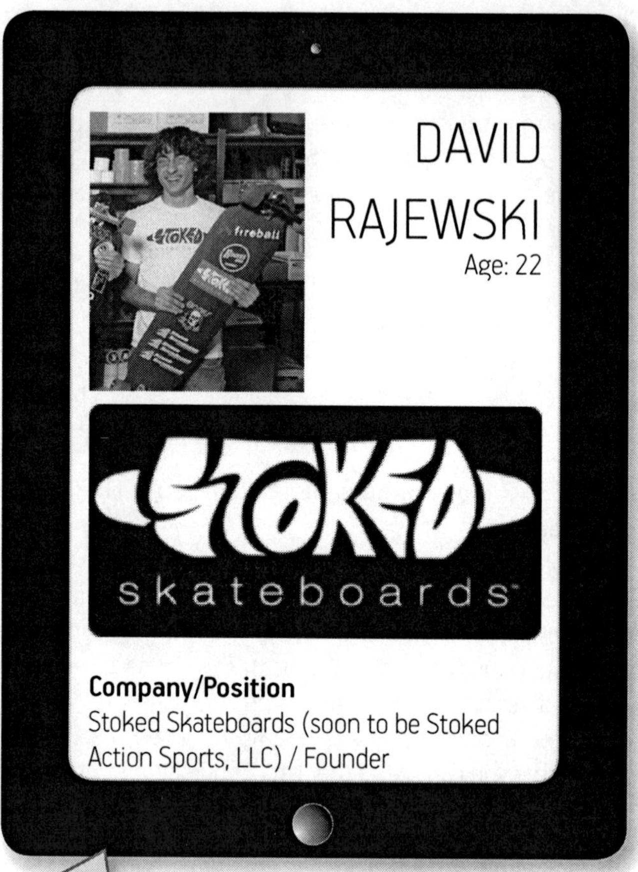

David Rajewski started his first business in highschool at the age of 16. Living in Southern California David's greatest passion has always been skateboarding. This young entrepreneur turned a $1,000 loan into a million dollar skateboarding company. Stoked Skateboards is a skate board company that is all about spreading the stoke. Beginning with the support of Loaded Boards, Stoked was founded around great customer service, excellent products, and the need to spread the stoke of boarding to as many people as possible. The Skate Stoked Team, an innovative new way to spread the love of boarding, was made just for this purpose and causes the sport to thrive by reaching out to more and more new skaters. Dedicated day in and day out to superb customer satisfaction, Stoked grew from its humble beginnings into one of the most recognized specialty skate shops.

» **Give a detailed description of the work that you do. What are your job responsibilities?**

My main roles are to manage the day to day, come up with an overall business strategy, make sure we are on budget, find new opportunities, and maintain the business.

» **What made you think of your idea?**

I wanted to buy a car and didn't have any money! I liked skateboards and thought I could sell them. I just looked for what was missing and did what I thought people would like.

» **How did you get started?**

Yahoo Small Business offered a website platform for $30 a month. I called manufacturers until one would sell to me. Once I got one, I was in business!

» **What were the biggest challenges that you encountered?**

I was pretty intimidated by speaking with companies at 16 years old. I had to hide my age a bit, but ultimately, no one really cared as long as I followed the rules and stuff was selling. My biggest challenge was overcoming my own mental blocks. I still feel that's my biggest challenge.

» **What would you say is your greatest accomplishment along on the way?**

Getting people stoked! I love knowing someone else also loves the business I love.

» **How did you get into this job? How easy or difficult it was for you to venture into this business?**

I got this job because I wanted to start an online retail store. It was actually pretty easy to venture into skateboards, but I think getting into any business can be easy if you come at it in the right way.

» **Have you always been interested in this kind of work?**

Yes, I have always had an entrepreneurial/business kind of mindset.

» **What has this experience been like? Any interesting points you would like to share?**

It has been an awesome experience, but it isn't without it's faults. Sometimes I feel like I gave up a "normal" college experience or a "normal" high school experience for this job. However, looking back, I wouldn't change anything. Starting young allows you to make your mistakes early. Usually your mistakes are much easier to manage, so you get more of a lesson rather than the pain. This can be very valuable.

» **What is the most challenging part of your job and why?**

The hardest part for me has been the juggle of social life, school, and job. It seems you just get to choose two. Try to do more than two and something else starts to suffer.

» **What fulfillment do you get from your job?**

SO MUCH FULFILLMENT! Sometimes I wake up in the morning cranky and not super stoked to head into the shop. However, I always feel motivated and passionate when I leave at the end of the day. It is energizing to build something bigger than yourself.

» **What important lessons have you learned in the process of establishing your company?**

- The people you hire are everything. My professors for my business plan class say to hire slow and fire fast. This is a lesson I needed to learn sooner.

- Too much inventory will eat your cash and then destroy you.

- Research your product until you are absolutely certain it is perfect for production. Then research it again. And again. And again. Then go to production.

» **What do you think helped you the most in your success?**

The people around me. I've been blessed to be surrounded by great mentors and teachers.

» **Where and how do you see yourself five or ten years from now?**

- Building the world's largest action sports retailer.

- Having a great wife and family.

- Traveling the world.

» **How do you spend money – business or personal-wise?**

- Business-wise, I spend my money to make more money. Especially when times are tough, I ask myself will this dollar I'm spending bring in ten more?

- Personal-wise, I travel, go out with friends, ride skateboards, and race my car.

» **What is the most important advice you would give to other entrepreneurs?**

There is a quote from Lee Iacocca that goes "We are continually faced by great opportunities brilliantly disguised as insoluble problems." I think this is such a great way of looking at the world. See everything as opportunities instead of problems. If you can't take advantage of the opportunity just yet, let it sit and ripen in your mind. Something will come to you.

 www.stokedskateboards.com

 @skatestoked

 www.facebook.com/StokedSkateboards

Ashley is from New Hampshire, and is a bright young entrepreneur. While still in college Ashley turned her passion for fashion into a growing business. A La Plage is an adventurous beach/island inspired jewelry company. These unique, colorful pieces are perfect for any age and are a fun and easy way to channel your inner island spirit, no matter what season you're in.

» **Give a detailed description of the work that you do. What are your job responsibilities?**

Design and maintain website, put together collections and maintain inventory, marketing, finances, scheduling events and trunk shows, creating a loyal customer base, branding our product

» **What made you think of your idea? How did you get started?**

I have always grown up in retail. My parents have always owned gifts shops and things of the sort so I guess it was in my blood! During my sophomore year of college at the University of New Hampshire I got inspired by one of our family friends who opened her own boutique in Maui. When I went to visit her I was so inspired but what she did and how far she had come by following her passion. So when I returned back to campus I decided to follow my passion and start my own online business. I love fashion so starting out in the jewelry business was perfect! Within the first month of starting my college roommate at the time and my best friend (Caleigh Adler) was just as passionate as I was about the company and the potential it had to take off so I decided to take her on as a partner. From that point on the two of us worked together to build A La Plage from the ground up.

» **What were the biggest challenges that you encountered?**

Starting off from scratch I would say the biggest challenge at first was money. It was hard to not make a profit for a while at the beginning. But we held on to our dreams and goals and before we knew it we were going above and beyond what we expected. Another challenge I would say would be expanding the business to different demographics and having product that will cater to a wide variety of women.

» **What would you say is your greatest accomplishment along on the way?**

I would say just being recognized and having people recognize your product and your company, and seeing the business grow into places you never thought possible!

» **How did you get into this job? How easy or difficult it was for you to venture into this business?**

I was inspired by my family and friends. I had an unreal support system. My family has always supported me in everything I have done. They were more than happy to see that I wanted to turn my dream into a reality and helped me in any way they could to make it happen for me! Because of this it made the venture into the business much easier. It was still challenging at times but I can't explain how good it feels to have support from family and friends along the way, no matter what happens.

» **Have you always been interested in this kind of work?**

Yes, like I said I have grown up in the retail business but I have always LOVED fashion!

» **What has this experience been like? Any interesting points you would like to share?**

It has been amazing. I honestly would have to say that I have grown up a lot with the business. Having this while being in college is challenging and frustrating at times because it's hard to have a social life all the time like other people do, so it took me a while to find that balance. But I do have to say making that sacrifice has made me into a better person today.

» **What is the most challenging part of your job and why?**

Not really having a set schedule and doing it whenever I can between classes and school. Also finding a balance between A La Plage time and free time.

» **What fulfillment do you get from your job?**

Seeing customers happy and pleased with our product and service. We try to focus our company not only on just the product itself but the idea of being confident and feeling good in whatever you wear. It's about making a statement hence our motto "be bold, be sexy, be classy." It's important to feel & look confident in your look, especially in the business world, so when we see women doing that and more importantly doing it with our product it is really rewarding.

» **What important lessons have you learned in the process of establishing your company?**

Follow your dream but be open to small changes and adjustments along the way, Whenever things don't seem to work out... it's crucial not to give up and to take a deep breath and come up with a new goal or a new way to get what you want, Pay very close attention to the little things, stay organized, be responsible with spending, make sacrifices, and the importance of making a decision and never looking back, ALWAYS move forward and learn from your mistakes in the past.

» **What do you think helped you the most in your success?**

Having supportive friends and family and having an amazing business partner and best friend

» **Where and how do you see yourself five or ten years from now?**

I have a goal to open up a clothing boutique

» **What is the most important advice you would give to other entrepreneurs?**

Follow your dreams and stick with it. It may seem close to impossible at times but NEVER give up. If you want something bad enough, and work your ass off to get it then you will make it happen!

 www.alaplagejewelry.com

 @AshleyRozumek

 www.facebook.com/alaplagejewelry

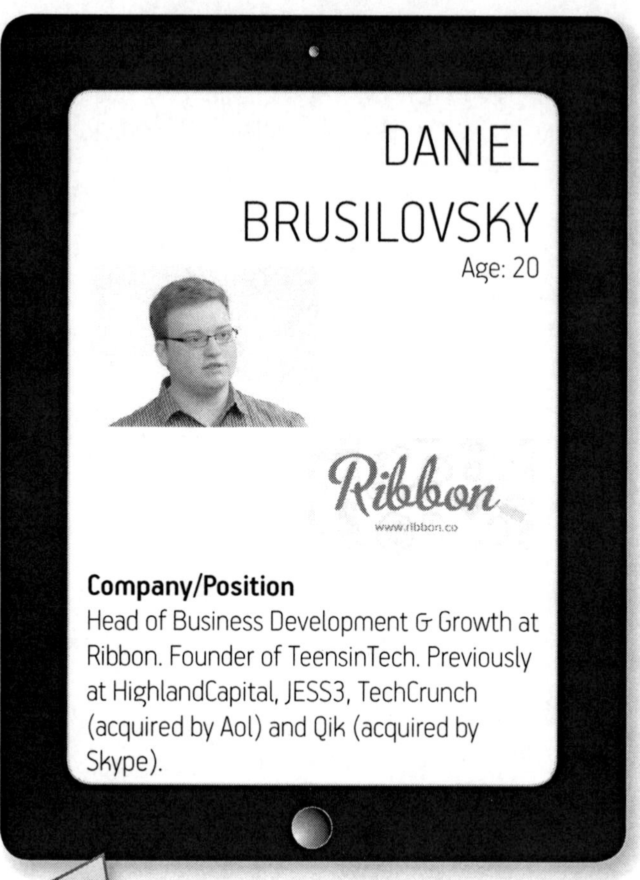

Daniel started his first successful company at age 15, TeensinTech. Daniel is a smart young entrepreneur making a big name for himself in Silicon Valley. Daniel is now a writer, speaker, CEO. Currently working as head of development at Ribbon, Ribbon makes selling across multiple platforms easy. Sell instantly inside Facebook, Twitter, and your own website! Ribbon lets you list your product to create a beautiful showcase page. Ribbon supports all types of products from physical and digital goods to services. From T-shirts, mp3s to tutoring, Ribbon lets you sell with ease and elegance. Prior to Ribbon, Daniel spent time at Highland Capital Partners, JESS3, TechCrunch, was on the founding team of Qik (acquired by Skype), and started his own company, Teens in Tech Labs.

» **What is the most important advice you would give to other entrepreneurs?**

To never start a company or project for the sake of making money. Do something because you're passionate about it, and want to change something for the better. Not to make a quick buck.

» **What important lessons have you learned in the process of establishing your company?**

One of the most important lessons I learned was to surround yourself with people that not only you can trust, but can learn from, especially in the early days of any company. These are people you're going to be spending a lot of time with, and you want to make sure the relationship is strong.

» **Give a detailed description of the work that you do. What are your job responsibilities?**

Besides Teens in Tech, I run business development and growth at Ribbon, a payments company in San Francisco. No two days are ever the same, but I do spend a lot of time in meetings. That's always fun. :)

» **How did you get started?**

Growing up in Silicon Valley, I found myself always surrounded by technology and people in the industry. I joined a startup in December 2007 called Qik. While at Qik, I was going to a lot of events and realized I was always the youngest in the room. I wanted to meet others who were interested in tech who were young, and that's where the idea for Teens in Tech came from.

» **What would you say is your greatest accomplishment along on the way?**

Founding Teens in Tech, and starting the Teens in Tech Conference and the Teens in Tech Incubator is one of the biggest accomplishments. We've had an impact on young people that they wouldn't have gotten in other ways, and that makes me proud.

 www.ribbon.co

 @danielbru

 www.facebook.com /ribbon

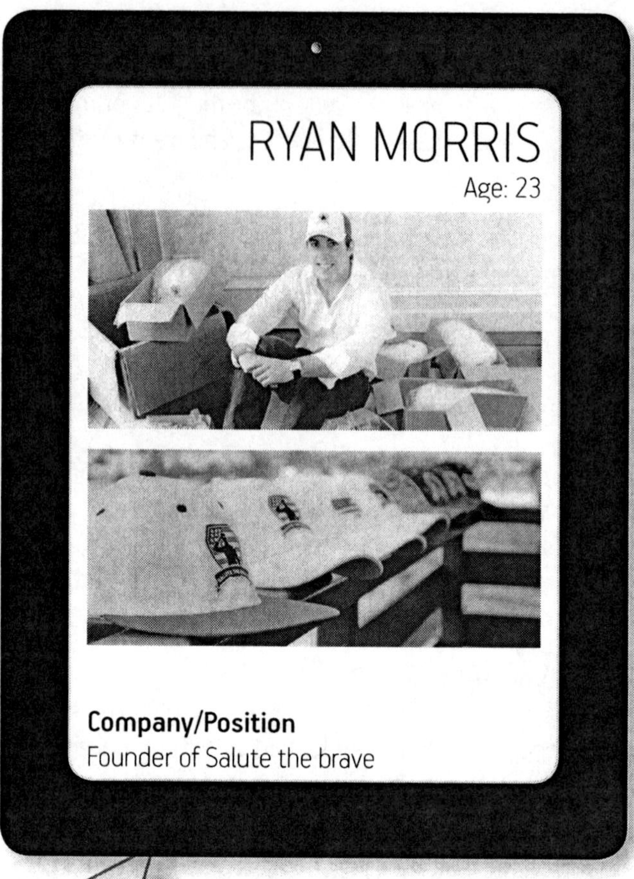

Ryan Morris is a successful entrepreneur who started his first business in college. Not only does he have a big heart, Ryan's company is all about working for a greater cause. Salute The Brave is a clothing line designed to give back to the men and women serving the United States of America in the armed forces. For every Salute The Brave purchased, one is then donated in a care package as a part of the "be a hero, for a hero" business model. All of the donated items have the words "free to be because of me" on the back, which serves as a thank you to the troops for their service and sacrifice to the United States. Salute The Brave has partnered with Operation Gratitude, which is a care package giving organization that sends 100,000 care packages overseas to the troops annually. Salute The Brave donates products and notes inside of the care packages to serve as a reminder to the troops that the folks back at home are behind them and support their willingness to service our great nation. It is a simple way to say "thank you" to our real heroes.

» **Give a detailed description of the work that you do. What are your job responsibilities?**

Managing everything, making sure our brand continues to grow and we continue to give back as much as possible and making sure that each day is a productive day.

» **What made you think of your idea?**

I always wanted to get into clothing and e commerce. I wanted to give back to the troops and I was able to talk to some United States veterans and the fact that they felt unappreciated made me want to do more to help them and so I figured out a way to combine the fact that I wanted to get into fashion and wanted to help the troops. I used Tom Shoes business model and went from there.

» **How did you get started?**

I found some manufactures got bunch of samples, and once I got the samples I asked all my friends what they thought and I got a lot of feedback, and then I figured out what the most successful products we could sell, and launched May 6th 2011.

» **What were the biggest challenges that you encountered?**

Driving traffic to the website. Keeping a level head. Staying motivated and passionate when things didn't always go well, and expanding the brand nationally.

» **What would you say is your greatest accomplishment along on the way?**

Making a difference in the lives of the veterans and the troops overseas.

» **How did you get into this job? How easy or difficult it was for you to venture into this business?**

You got to find your own niche, and your own customer market. Customers drive a business so anyone looking at starting a business you have to look at your customers. Identifying our customers, and identifying how we are going to reach those customers.

» **What has this experience been like? Any interesting points you would like to share?**

I think seeing people around town and seeing people wear the products is very gratifying, knowing what we have made has been successful. Hearing people talk about our products who have seen a veteran get a care package from us is defiantly a high point.

» **What important lessons have you learned in the process of establishing your company?**

In the end the customer is going to make or break a company, listening to their feedback and scaling a business off what information they have to offer is the most important thing. That whole customers always right thing is true.

» **What do you think helped you the most in your success?**

Being a college kid actually helped because I was able to be around my customers at all times being with other college kids, and having a mentor is also very helpful.

» **Where and how do you see yourself five or ten years from now?**

Doing what makes me happy and something that changes whatever industry I am in.

» **What is the most important advice you would give to other entrepreneurs?**

Don't let anyone tell you that you can't do anything. I had tons and tons of people telling me that a 21 year old college kid won't be able to start a company out of his dorm room and if I had listened to them I wouldn't be here today without that experience and without this company. Ignore your naysayers and always believe in yourself.

 www.salutethebrave.com

 @SaluteThebrave

 www.facebook.com/SaluteTheBrave

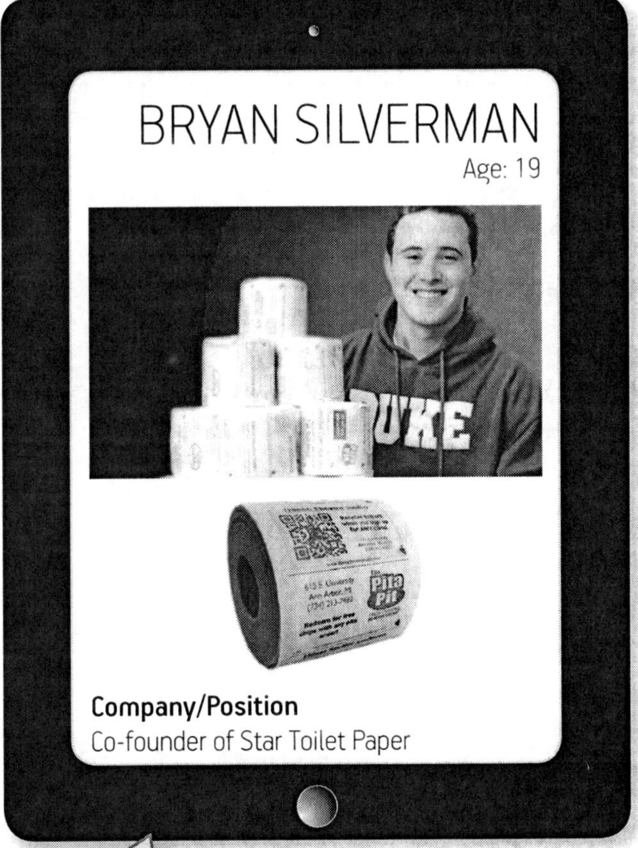

Bryan is a college student at Duke University with a very creative sense of business. While still in school Bryan and his brother started a company known as Star Toilet Paper. Star Toilet Paper is a unique advertising company that advertises on toilet paper. Star Toilet Paper is quickly becoming a leader in the field of unique advertising. By utilizing toilet paper as medium for advertising the brothers have created an exciting new option for small businesses that is succeeding at what most other forms of traditional advertising have failed to do; namely, getting noticed.

» **Give a detailed description of the work that you do. What are your job responsibilities?**

As a co-founder of a startup, I don't think I can pinpoint one thing I do. Compared to my brother, I am probably more a part of the PR and he is more behind the scenes, sales guy. however, as in any startup, it is necessary to wear many hats. I enjoy what I do and it is great that if I am not great at something, I get to learn through experience.

» **What made you think of your idea?**

My brother actually thought of the idea. He was in the bathroom, on his phone, just like everyone else is. It was an idea he wrote down in his phone and just kind of left for a little. Then he brought the idea to me and at first, I honestly thought he was crazy. However, we did some market research and realized that it is definitely a feasible idea.

» **How did you get started?**

A lot of work and a lot of cold calls. It was about a year and a half of market research, legal work, and patent searching. Eventually we started making sales called and only after about 2 to 3 months did we get our first advertiser.

» **What were the biggest challenges that you encountered?**

One of the biggest things that we encounter is the stigma associated with advertising on toilet paper. However, after people are able to get past the initial hesitation, they realize that advertising on toilet paper is a unique, cost-effective way to reach their desired target audience. Second, for me, I had a difficult time getting past the first "no" I heard. It wasn't that it took me a long time, it was more about an unexpected experience. However, I soon came to realize that I would be hearing "no" often and I had to take each one in stride and use it as motivation to get closer to hearing that next "yes."

» **What would you say is your greatest accomplishment along on the way?**

There are company accomplishments and personal accomplishments. As a company, the first venue I worked on was the Port Chester-Rye Brook Public Library, the local library in my hometown. It was great to see that come to fruition in that it was the first project I had made sales calls on and it only made it better that it was my hometown. My best personal accomplishment was definitely winning Entrepreneur Magazine's College Entrepreneur of the Year.

» **How did you get into this job? How easy or difficult it was for you to venture into this business?**

The way my brother said it once, that definitely epitomizes the truth of entrepreneurship, is that I have caught the "entrepreneurial bug." I was a senior in high school and in the beginning of my college career, so the notion of innovation wasn't too unique to me. However, something as unique as advertising on toilet paper is certainly not something that is "normal" by any means.

» **Have you always been interested in this kind of work?**

In advertising on toilet paper? I don't think so. However, as I stated above, once I caught the entrepreneurial bug, it is hard not to think in a manner that you can always innovate and always improve something, no matter how "old" of a solution it is. Furthermore, I have developed a love for toilet paper. Something that not too many people would say, but I definitely love toilet paper and love being known as the "toilet paper guy."

» **What has this experience been like? Any interesting points you would like to share?**

It has been unbelievable. Not many 19-year-olds can say they started a business, let alone one that has been this successful. I have had numerous publicity pieces written about me, some even on the front cover of newspapers. I have been called a "hometown hero" and had people call me an inspiration. I find this all to be a huge honor and to be very humbling and an honestly surreal experience. It is almost indescribable, both the publicity we have been getting as well as the success we have been achieving. Despite all of this, it is essential to remember that improvements can always be made and you can always get better.

» **What is the most challenging part of your job and why?**

I would say the long hours. However, this is normally associated with a negative connotation. And sometimes I do get tired and exhausted from the work. However, it is all work that I love and that I have a passion for. Thus, the long hours I put in I am fortunate enough to enjoy every waking moment.

» **What fulfillment do you get from your job?**

There are a number of reasons I get fulfillment. First of all, and this is a quote by Confucius that one of my high school teachers had on her wall - "Choose a job you love and you will never work a day in your life." I definitely live by that and, as I said before, I love what I do. Second, I am fortunate enough to have amazing people on my team who I work with every day. Finally, I am able to meet amazing people along the way. Whether these are other entrepreneurs, our clients, or just people who have said they love the idea, I love what they say to me and how I get to know so many new people on a personal level.

» **What important lessons have you learned in the process of establishing your company?**

One thing, that I touched on above, is the value of hearing no. There are a few things that our team thinks of when we hear no. First of all, we don't let it stop or hinder us. Second, we look at what we did wrong and how we can improve it. Whether that is improve ourselves, improve the cold call script, or make a suggestion to the team, it is essential to learn from hearing no. Finally, we use no's as motivation to prove these naysayers wrong. Each no we think of as that much closer to hearing the next yes.

» **What do you think helped you the most in your success?**

There are a few things. First of all, my parents have always fostered an environment where if we wanted something, it wasn't just going to be given to us. We had to not only work to get it, but had to take advantage of others to whom we could ask questions. Second, both my brother and myself have been able to take advantage of the resources the university has to offer. Whether this is networking, office space, or the many other resources a university has to offer, we have been able to tap into them to take advantage. Duke University (where I am studying neuroscience as a member of the Class of 2015), Durham, University of Michigan-Ann Arbor (where my brother graduated with a degree in philosophy as a member of the Class of 2012), and Ann Arbor have been unbelievable

» **Where and how do you see yourself five or ten years from now?**

I see myself in one of 2 places. Ideally, I either want to be working on Star Toilet Paper or have the legacy of Star Toilet Paper. When I say legacy, I mean two things. 1 - we have been a successful company that has either successfully exited or continues to be successful. 2 - I want to be someone who is able to help others the way others have helped me. The entrepreneurial community is a great one in that those that have succeeded know they could not have done it without the help of those who succeeded before them. Because I have learned so much and plan on learning so much more, I want to be able to help those that come after me.

» **How do you spend money – business or personal-wise?**

Very stingy. I have learned how far a few dollars can go. Whether that is in my personal life or in our business, we are sure to spend in as lean a way as possible.

» **What is the most important advice you would give to other entrepreneurs?**

Go for it! There are so many crazy ideas, and so many people that think they have a cool idea that they don't bring to fruition. However, I started this company as a 17-year-old. We print advertisements and coupons on toilet paper.

The crazy ideas are the ones that disrupt the status quo and that are most successful. I would also tell them not to be afraid to ask questions and ask for advice. Without the help of others, we would not be where we are now. There are others that have the experience and are happy to help and if you don't ask questions, you will never know the answers. Don't be afraid, be ambitious.

 www.startoiletpaper.com

 @bryanstartp

 www.facebook.com/startoiletpaper

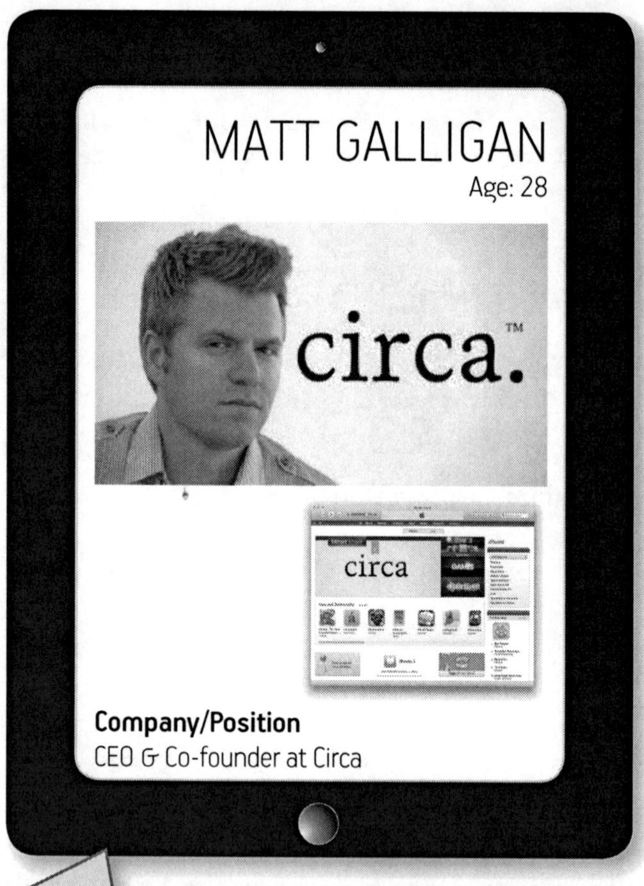

Matt is an innovative, cool, young entrepreneur, with great ideas. Matt came up with an idea to make reading the news easier and more enjoyable for users. More and more people are relying on their phones as their primary source of news, yet the content is presented in ways that make it annoying to read. Rather than shoehorning existing content into a new environment, Circa is creating the first born-on-mobile news experience, delivering it in a format native to mobile devices, with an experience intuitive to mobile users. Through comprehensive yet concise news updates paired with a clean, simple mobile experience, Circa redefines how news is produced, delivered, and consumed. Circa is news, re-imagined.

» **Give a detailed description of the work that you do. What are your job responsibilities?**

My role in the company (Circa) is CEO. Typically that work means that I'm managing the business, and making sure that we're always on target to meet our goals. But seeing as how we're still a small company, I still do quite a bit of other work. That includes:

Product design: I come up with a lot of the features that Circa builds. Typically I will have an idea that I will sketch out or discuss with the team, and then make sure that it's built according to my thoughts.

Fundraising: I have to always make sure we've got money in the bank. So far we've raised about $1.6m and that's been entirely through my fundraising efforts and bringing on angel investors.

Hiring: This is one of the hardest parts of the job – identifying and interviewing great candidates. A CEO's job is to make sure there's always great talent working for the company. It's tough, but it's worth it when we bring some great people on board.

Coding & Design: Sometimes we're so slammed with stuff to get done that I'll even jump in and start designing and coding stuff. This is fairly rare, but definitely still part of my job.

Keeping the beer fridge stocked: I think you'll get this one...

» **What made you think of your idea?**

I absolutely love learning, and soaking up information. But I noticed that when I started to rely more on my mobile phone that I wasn't getting my news as much as before. I think it's because articles are just so long, and when I'm on my phone, I want to focus on things that I can get through fast. That's how Circa was started...I wanted to be able to read news in a really fast, succinct, but comprehensive way.

» **How did you get started?**

Ben Huh (Cheezburger Network) and I got together and discussed what we thought would be helpful to build a news product. Then I went around to some friends and trusted colleagues to vet the idea. After which I raised a bit of money so that we could kick things off...

» **What were the biggest challenges that you encountered?**

One of the biggest challenges so far for me has been hiring great people. We have built such an incredible team so far where everyone is very talented and gets along famously. As a result, the bar has been set very very high for any subsequent hires. Finding the perfect fit is incredibly difficult, but I wouldn't lower our standards at all.

» **What would you say is your greatest accomplishment along on the way?**

I'd say two things: building an amazing team and enabling them to develop a fantastic product. We've got amazing reviews in the App Store and people really love it...which makes the team feel great.

» **How did you get into this job? How easy or difficult it was for you to venture into this business?**

I started Circa because I just wanted it to exist. I wasn't going to wait around for someone else to build it. I suppose that's what makes up an Entrepreneur. A few years back when I started my first business it wasn't because I wanted to work for myself, but rather because I felt like there were needs in the world that weren't being fulfilled and I wanted to tackle them. That desire has continued through today and will likely last my entire life.

Have you always been interested in this kind of work?

Absolutely. Even when I was a kid I was trying to build things, and while I wasn't necessarily starting businesses around them I think I always had a great curiosity for what I might be able to do.

» **What has this experience been like? Any interesting points you would like to share?**

This particular company has been fascinating. I've never been in news before, and to jump into a brand new market where it's existed hundreds of years before you is amazing. It's also incredibly humbling. I think a lot of people might treat me as a "young whippersnapper" but ultimately I just feel like I need to bring some of my unique perspective to the table entirely unhindered by the previous years of journalism and news. That's worked to our advantage as we've come up with some really novel stuff.

» **What is the most challenging part of your job and why?**

Along the lines of question 4, I'd say it's hiring as well as making sure we're always doing the right thing. It's easy to just stuff a bunch of features into a product, but it should always require an incredible amount of thought to make sure you're doing the right thing.

» **What fulfillment do you get from your job?**

The satisfaction that I might be a tiny part of making peoples' lives better. We constantly get reviews in the App Store that talk about how someone is able to stay more informed in the news because of Circa, and that makes me insanely happy.

» **What was it like when you realized you made your first million?**

This was back in 2008 when I had sold my first company, Socialthing. The first thing that went through my head was that I could help my parents pay off their debt they accumulated raising two kids, and help my brother with his school tuition. Family is the #1 most important thing to me and helping them out was the best thing I could have possibly thought to do.

» **What important lessons have you learned in the process of establishing your company?**

Never get too comfortable. Always think ahead. Always question the decisions you've made and make sure you're on the bleeding edge.

» **What do you think helped you the most in your success?**

That I'm open to advice. Some entrepreneurs can be incredibly stubborn and find themselves stuck when the things they thought were brilliant don't work out. Instead, I think it's important to be humble, seek advice, and implement the right course of action despite if you came up with it or not.

» **Where and how do you see yourself five or ten years from now?**

Building more products.

» **How do you spend money – business or personal-wise?**

Business: as pragmatically as possible. That doesn't mean I'm super lean and stringent, I just try to spend money on the right things. Sometimes that means having comfortable chairs for employees, and sometimes that means having tasty beer for them when they wind their day down.

Personal: I'd say my two biggest expenditures beyond the average bills are clothes and gadgets.

» **What is the most important advice you would give to other entrepreneurs?**

Stay humble, stay focused, and hope you're never ever satisfied with the status quo.

 www.cir.ca

 @mg

 www.facebook.com/mattgalligan

ALEXA CARLIN

Age: 21

Company/Position

Founder and Creative Thinker of Hello Perfect

Alexa is an inspirational entrepreneur for all women. She founded a company known as Hello Perfect. Hello Perfect is an inspirational fashion blog advocating that the challenge in life is not to become perfect, it's accepting that you already are. We are redefining society's definition of the word "perfect" and inspiring people with the confidence they need to accomplish their dreams.

» **How did you get started?**

I started by just diving right in! I started up a website on GoDaddy (now I use Wordpress) and wrote down every single idea I had in a journal. After that it was just a step by step process to begin writing blog posts, researching the industry and really trying to figure out my target market niche.

» **What were the biggest challenges that you encountered?**

For me the biggest challenge was actually having too many ideas. I was overwhelmed with everything I wanted to accomplish right that second that a lot of the times I ended up getting nothing done! You have to really plan out the steps and your growth process and know that it's better to focus on one thing than try to do a million.

» **What would you say is your greatest accomplishment along on the way?**

My greatest accomplishment along the way is gaining the confidence in myself to be vulnerable and keep on going no matter what anyone else says or thinks.

» **Have you always been interested in this kind of work?**

I've always wanted to make a difference in others lives and I've always aspired to work in the fashion industry. It was the challenge to really find something where I can fulfill all of my passions, so I created something that would.

» **What fulfillment do you get from your job?**

The fulfillment I get with working on Hello Perfect is something I would never be able to really explain. I am accomplishing my dream while working to help others see their full potential and accomplish their own dream; it's the best job in the world.

» **What do you think helped you the most in your success?**

My drive and passion has helped me the most in my success.

» **What is the most important advice you would give to other entrepreneurs?**

The most important advice I would give to other entrepreneurs is to make sure you love what you are doing because creating your own company takes up almost all of your time and energy, especially in the early stages. If you aren't passionate about what you do, it'll never work.

 www.helloperfect.com

 @AlexaRoseCarlin

 www.facebook.com/pages/Hello-Perfect/221033867928970

Kirk is young technology entrepreneur. While still in school Kirk started a successful company known as Scan. Scan is creating disruptive apps that connect the real world with the digital universe in fun and innovative ways. Through QR code, NFC, and other technologies, Scan brings social media, lead generation, and mobile commerce to life through real world "like", "follow", and even "buy" buttons. Companies can easily use Scan's tools to create these custom experiences for their customers.

» **Give a detailed description of the work that you do. What are your job responsibilities?**

I wear many hats. I manage hiring, firing, product features, legal, company roadmap, accounting, support, and more.

» **What made you think of your idea?**

One of my friends from my university had the initial idea to do a site around QR codes and scanning, one thing led to another, and now we are a fully funded and operation company.

» **How did you get started?**

My friend Garrett designed the website and app, I built the website, and my other friend Ben built the app. We then applied to business plan competitions and were lucky enough to start winning them.

» **What were the biggest challenges that you encountered?**

The hardest and most important part of building a business is fighting to find amazing talent to add to the team.

» **What would you say is your greatest accomplishment along on the way?**

We recently passed 30 million installations of our app, which has been our greatest accomplishment so far.

» **How did you get into this job? How easy or difficult it was for you to venture into this business?**

I had free time in college to be able to work on fun projects with friends. Because I had other websites making money passively, it allowed me to spend time on these projects.

» **Have you always been interested in this kind of work?**

I have always loved technology and the Internet.

» **What has this experience been like? Any interesting points you would like to share?**

It has been a rollercoaster - some days you feel on top of the world, other days are incredibly difficult. Looking back, it is incredible to see how many seemingly small things have come together to make something much bigger.

» **What is the most challenging part of your job and why?**

Finding amazing talent to join the team. Many people are looking for work, but most of the best talent is already highly compensated and engaged in other work. Tracking down these people and converting them to our team is a difficult undertaking.

» **What fulfillment do you get from your job?**

I pressed a button the other day that released something our team worked hard on to millions of people. That was awesome.

» **What was it like when you realized you made your first million?**

Right now all of the founders are paper millionaires, meaning our stock in our company is worth millions of dollars if we are able to execute well over the next few years. Ask me again when we become cash millionaires (actually have the money in our accounts).

» **What important lessons have you learned in the process of establishing your company?**

Starting your own business is one of the most stressful things you can do, but it also one of the most rewarding.

» **What do you think helped you the most in your success?**

Having a supportive wife that loves me.

» **Where and how do you see yourself five or ten years from now?**

Hopefully we will have built Scan to a point where it is incredibly successful and stable. I am looking forward to my first son who is due June 9, 2013.

» **How do you spend money – business or personal-wise?**

I'm pretty frugal, but most of my expenses are on food, home, and electronics.

» **What is the most important advice you would give to other entrepreneurs?**

If you want to build a tech company, develop a strong technical skill, whether it be programming, design, or online marketing. These skills are best developed by working on personal projects that you are passionate about.

www.scan.me

@kirkouimet

www.facebook.com/scanpage

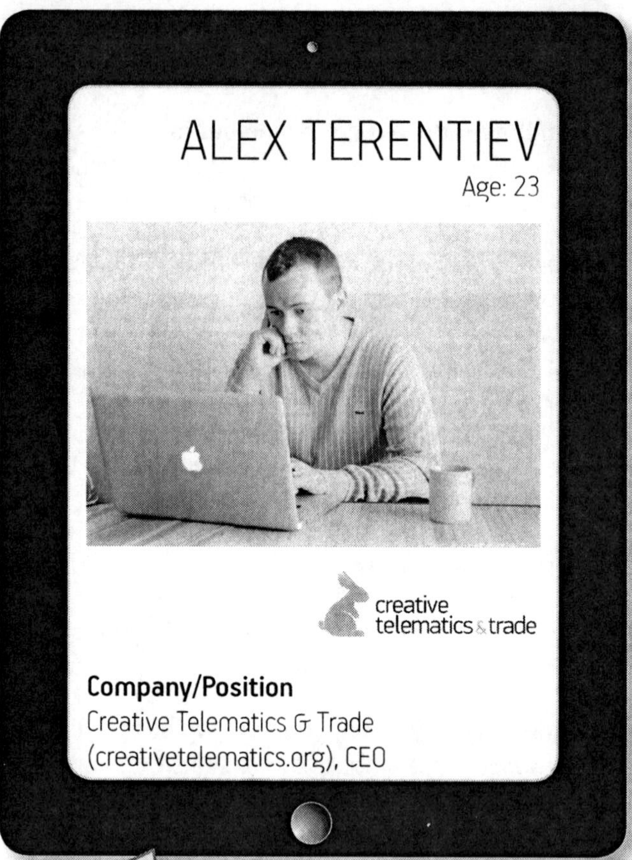

Alex Terentiev was born in Moscow, educated as a journalist-politologist, and now lives in Prague. Creative Telematics & Trade has been consulting those who produce and sell services in the sphere of telematics (webhosting, domain names), marketing (SEO and copywriting), design (graphical design, webdesign and typography) and IT business.

» **Give a detailed description of the work that you do. What are your job responsibilities?**

I'm a CEO, I hire staff and manage with tasks which are connected with our main billing & sales issues, corporate strategy and creative decisions.

» **What made you think of your idea?**

I was 17 and I wanted to find an ability to earn money and become an independent person.

» **How did you get started?**

The first serious project is a hosting company (NKVD.pro — http://nkvd.pro — right on March we are going to launch a new website of it). I earned my first $50 as a forum designer and spent them to register a domain name for my future hosting company. About half a year after I hired the first man as a Technical Support Manager — he is still working with me, now he is a Senior Technical Director.

» **What were the biggest challenges that you encountered?**

In 2009 during the Great Recession we started being involved in dedicated servers market. Other hosting companies which were older broke. It was really hard to attract customers, to make them believe we are able to become a trustful member of the Russian-speaking telematics market, but now, 4 years after, I see we have successfully done it.

» **What would you say is your greatest accomplishment along on the way?**

In 2011 I got a good offer from a bigger company which would like to buy our brand and our customers. I was thinking about starting something new and was kind of tired of hosting business. But I declined this offer and never regretted about it.

» **How did you get into this job? How easy or difficult it was for you to venture into this business?**

I worked hard and believed in success, I have never given an easy time to myself.

» **Have you always been interested in this kind of work?**

I graduated from a high school as a political journalist and when I was going to enter the Higher School of Economics in 2006 I had no idea that I will work for telematics sphere. The interest came during the work.

» **What has this experience been like? Any interesting points you would like to share?**

One of my colleagues and a very good friend of mine believes: if a person works hard 24/7/365, the success will inevitably come. I do my best to follow this simple rule.

» **What is the most challenging part of your job and why?**

Business competition is the most interesting thing in my job. It is the best motivation at the same time.

» **What fulfillment do you get from your job?**

Interest and money for my non-commercial projects and investment.

» **What was it like when you realized you made your first million?**

My first million was in rubles, of course, it's about 33 000 USD, so that's why I have something to aim at.

» **What important lessons have you learned in the process of establishing your company?**

Work only with the people you can trust.

» **What do you think helped you the most in your success?**

Lack of laziness.

» **Where and how do you see yourself five or ten years from now?**

I don't like predicting and guessing.

» **How do you spend money – business or personal-wise?**

Business. When I spend on personal things it is mostly travelling.

» **What is the most important advice you would give to other entrepreneurs?**

Let me quote Artemy Lebedev, the best Russian designer. "How to motivate yourself to start doing something? In no way, stay in the ass".

www.creativetelematics.org
www.terentiev.ru

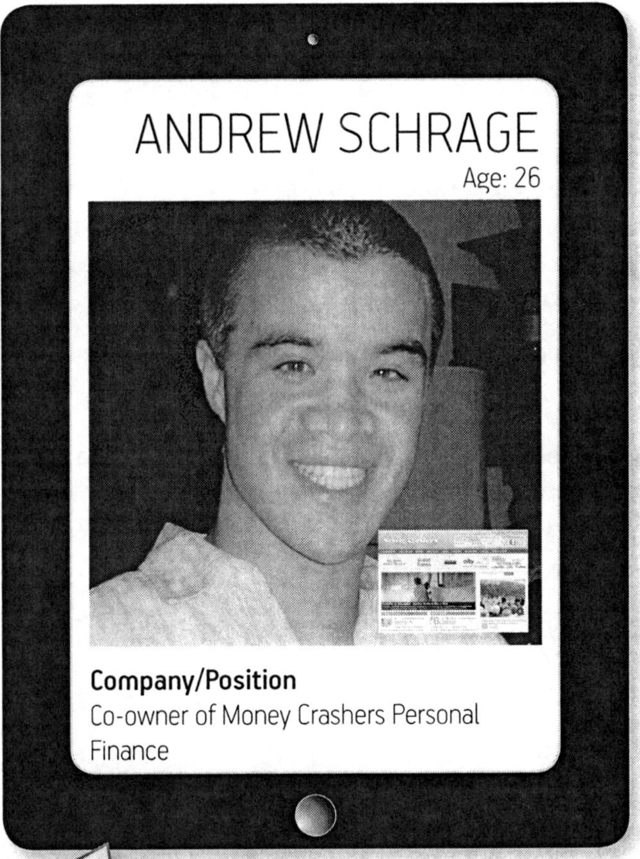

This knowledgeable entrepreneur helps people of all ages make better financial decisions. With a degree in economics, Andrew was tired of working for someone else, so he decided to start his own company. Money Crashers Personal Finance is a resource that strives to educate readers about how to better manage their money and improve their financial fitness. The site works to provide readers of all ages and background with the resources and educations to achieve their financial goals and prosper. Topics covered include budgeting, getting out of debt, credit card advice, starting a small business, how to extreme coupon, and preparing for retirement. Find out how you can better manage your ***money*** and build wealth. Learn more about topics like budgeting, investing, smart shopping, credit cards, and debt.

» **Give a detailed description of the work that you do. What are your job responsibilities?**

I am the owner and publisher of Money Crashers, a personal finance website. I am responsible for the day-to-day operations of the website.

» **What made you think of your idea?**

I studied finance in school, and it's something I've always been very passionate about. I like helping people as well, so the two ideas came together in the form of Money Crashers.

» **How did you get started?**

I launched my business while still working a regular day job.

» **What were the biggest challenges that you encountered?**

Some of the biggest challenges that most small business owners come up against are finding ways to save money and prevent over-spending, and effectively marketing the business.

» **What would you say is your greatest accomplishment along on the way?**

One of the greatest accomplishments an aspiring entrepreneur can make is the jump from working at a day job to working full-time for the small business he or she owns. There are risks involved and it takes a lot of courage, but for those who see things through, the benefits are tremendous.

» **How did you get into this job? How easy or difficult it was for you to venture into this business?**

Considering my collegiate background and some of my professional work experience, it really wasn't that difficult to break into the personal finance industry.

» **Have you always been interested in this kind of work?**

Yes, I became interested in economics and finances at a young age.

» **What has this experience been like? Any interesting points you would like to share?**

The experience has been great. Small business owners who are willing to put in the necessary time and hard work can begin to enjoy some significant advantages once the business becomes established. You can delegate many of your responsibilities, and as long as you manage your time well, you can actually work fewer hours.

» **What is the most challenging part of your job and why?**

Staying competitive and remaining relevant in social media is always a challenge. Most adept small business owners are already on board with social media, and it always seems like there's some new twist coming out that allows businesses to more effectively target their customers. The challenge lies in incorporating these new technologies in one's social media strategy.

» **What fulfillment do you get from your job?**

I know that at the end of the day, I'm helping people and making a difference in their lives. The economy has been rough for quite some time now, and people just don't have the money to spend like they used to. Knowing that I'm making things a bit easier for the people who subscribe to my website is very fulfilling.

» **What important lessons have you learned in the process of establishing your company?**

I learned that saving money is essential in the beginning if you're going to be successful, and jumping in the social media game is a must for anyone looking to effectively market their business.

» **What do you think helped you the most in your success?**

My work ethic. I've always been a hard (and smart) worker, and I know how to get a lot done in a short period of time. Time management is also another key to small business success.

» **Where and how do you see yourself five or ten years from now?**

I see myself continuing to run Money Crashers and always looking for ways to improve and innovate.

» **How do you spend money – business or personal-wise?**

I've always been frugal with my money, and for good reason. Being frugal with my business allows the business to thrive and be more profitable, and being frugal in my personal life allows me to save as much as I can so I can live the lifestyle of someone with a much higher income that I currently have. Also, whenever something comes along that I really want to purchase, it's nice to know I have the money in the bank to make it happen (though I might ultimately pass on the purchase).

» **What is the most important advice you would give to other entrepreneurs?**

Work hard, be consistent, and save every penny you can. As long as you're passionate about what you do, success should eventually come your way.

www.moneycrashers.com

@MoneyCrashers

www.facebook.com/MoneyCrashers

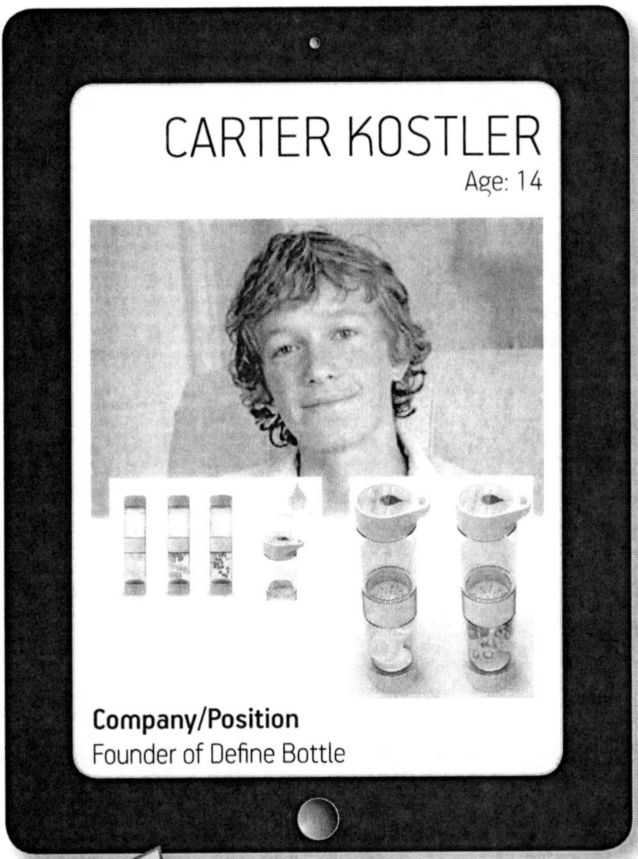

While still in high school Carter has focused his time on making the World a healthier place. Carter realized the affects of sugary drinks and in reaction to this created the Define Bottle. The Define Bottle is an elegantly designed, eco-friendly water bottle that allows you to take delicious, nutrient-rich, fruit-infused water ***to go***.

» **Give a detailed description of the work that you do. What are your job responsibilities?**

My name is Carter Kostler, I am 14 years old and I was born and raised in Virginia Beach, Virginia. My dream of creating a product and being an entrepreneur began in January of 2012 when I began formulating a concept in my mind to give people an alternative, healthy way to hydrate while on the go. From the outset, my goal was to improve the health of children and adults one drink at a time by providing the tools for a sustainable alternative to juice, soda and other sugary drinks that have contributed to the obesity and type 2 diabetes epidemic. Every day the negative impacts of soda and juice can be seen all around us. I personally have seen the effects on my friends and family.

» **What made you think of your idea?**

After watching the movie "super size me", I began to research the negative health effects of soda and juice. Diabetes and obesity sounded like terrible diseases and I desired to do something about it. I saw the need to make a sustainable, portable version of popular fruit infused water pitchers for people on the go. I am sure you are wondering where this idea came from.

Every day, my mother would cut up fresh strawberries, pineapples, kiwi, cucumber and place them into a large fruit infused water pitcher and store it in the refrigerator and drink it throughout the day. It was a natural, healthy way to flavor her water. However, when she would go out, she would grab a diet soda or a plastic water bottle. I asked her why she didn't take her fruit infused water with her on the go and she said there wasn't a really good way to do it. I did some research on my own and didn't see anything really great out there so I saw a void in the market, a solution to an epidemic and a chance to do something about it.With this in mind, I created the Define Bottle. The Define Bottle is a cool looking fruit infused water bottle to take on the go. I took the concept behind popular fruit infused water pitchers and made it portable, not to mention stylish. To help solve the obesity problem, you have to address the behaviors behind the disease. The connection between sugary drinks and obesity is clear. Empty calories from juice and soda are readily available and we need to give people of all ages the right tools to create a healthy alternative.

» **What do you think helped you the most in your success?**

From day one, I knew that I would need my parents support on the idea to even have a chance at this becoming a reality. Step one was to sketch some concepts, create a business plan the best I could, and pitch my idea to my parents. I was nervous to do this because although I thought it was a great idea and was really excited about it, I wasn't sure if my parents would agree.

I asked to call a family meeting and spent about an hour going over my concept with my parents. I explained why I thought it would be successful, how it would have an impact on people and why I needed their support. To my surprise they were very open to my idea and quickly became just as excited as I was. We started collaborating that day on how to bring this idea to market.

Taking a project from a dream or in my case some sketches to having a product in hand is a long journey and a lot of work. You have your path in your head and on paper but as you start taking the journey you quickly realize that the course is constantly changing. It is hard not to feel defeated when this happens but you need to be able to think smart and fast to get back on track. Most importantly you have to remain positive.

Once we were all on board we spent many days, nights and weekends thinking and sketching how the bottle would look and function. Once we nailed it, we contacted an intellectual property attorney to make sure that our idea was not already out there. This was the first hurdle. After our first of many modifications to come, we received a letter of patentability and we were given the green light to move forward. Once our patent was filed and we knew our idea was safe we started talking to designers on how to bring the Define Bottle to life. We filed for our patent to protect our concept and are currently patent pending. This alone was a great learning experience.

Having never done this before, we weren't sure about how the process would work. We did a lot of researching on the Internet when we were trying to find an industrial design firm to help us. We narrowed it down to a few based on products that they had already produced that were in a similar category to ours. We sent out a few emails explaining our project and what we were looking to do. Some companies never wrote back and the ones that did we interviewed to see who would be the best fit. We ended up forming a great relationship with an industrial design team out of Los Angeles. This was perhaps the most important relationship in our endeavor. We needed to be on the same page and be able to share our vision from 3000 miles away. Once we got the industrial design team on board it started to become fun. A Design Lab provided us with sketches and CAD designs that gave us an opportunity to see what our product would look like. During this phase we were hit with another hurdle. The design that we initially had planned was not able to be produced, so we had to make a few mechanical changes from a production standpoint.

Our original plan was to have one version of the bottle to be made out of glass and bamboo. However, after talking to a lot of people and doing some polling on Facebook and our website we came to realize that people wanted a non-glass alternative so they could take it to the gym or the pool. This meant that our design and production fees would double. It took a lot of thought and number crunching but we decided to move forward with it. We were on our way to success.

» **What would you say is your greatest accomplishment along on the way?**

Success can be measured in so many different ways especially when it comes to being an entrepreneur. Everyone defines success differently. Thus far I feel that I have had several defining moments of success. I first felt success having the backing of my parents support and having them believe in my idea. When I received the first prototype in the mail and held it in my hands I felt success that I was holding something that I created. It is early to define us as a financial success since we are still in our pre-launch phase. However, we turned to Indiegogo, a crowd-funding website, and exceeded our campaign goal by 60 percent. This made me realize that I created something that people wanted to buy and that felt like success. I was featured in Young Entrepreneur and Entrepreneur which was really awesome since Entrepreneur is one of our favorite magazines. I tend to revel in small successes like opening up my email and seeing that people are writing to me to purchase the bottle or requesting information to distribute it in other countries such as Chile, Australia and Sweden. Another success was meeting President Bill Clinton at the Health Matters Conference in Palm Springs. I donated 550 Define Bottles to the conference attendees in an effort to show them the bottle and how it can be used to improve health. Forbes wrote an amazing article about the concept and the President's response to it. My latest success is becoming a finalist in the Partnership for a Healthier America challenge to end childhood obesity. Thousands of people voted for my idea about using the bottle to improve health and I will present the idea in front of the First Lady, the Senate Majority Leader, and 1000 other important people in March, 2013.

There is a tremendous amount of learning to do with each stage of development. I have learned about patents, prototyping, crowd sourcing, packaging, and logistics. The patent process was probably the most difficult part to understand and my parents were actively involved with the work to get the patent filed. Design patents are easier to get, but do not have the strength to really protect an original idea. We filed for a utility patent, which required us to describe in detail how our product is different from those on the market. You also have to think about how others might attack your patent and how any changes to the product during development could impact the strength of the patent.

Right now we are in the tooling phase and this has been the most interesting so far. The pieces are coming to life and we are able to make changes to get the bottles just the way we envisioned them. I have learned how bottles are made and how things come into our country. The whole process has been fascinating.

The Internet has been an amazing resource during this process and made options available that never would be possible previously. We have worked with amazing people all over the world and we have never met them in person. Through e-mail, phone calls, and video messaging we have been able to conduct business with people we never could have found otherwise. A factory across the world will make a piece of the bottle and send a picture over and we can then discuss changes to the design right away. Crowd sourcing has been another learning experience. When we wanted to explore logo options we posted a request on Designcrowd.com and for very little money we had 30 designs to choose from in 24 hours from designers all over the world. As an entrepreneur, I have had to quickly learn about so many things that I never would have engaged with if I had not started a business.

There were days that were challenging and I began to have some doubts. It wasn't all great times. I contacted dozens of bloggers, editors, publications trying to get some buzz out there about my invention; I primarily received rejection but you had to keep on trying knowing that somebody would eventually see something in the product and give me a chance. I reached out to Entrepreneur and Young Entrepreneur and they both did a story on my idea and invention; those are both resources that I admired greatly. When times were tough I found a great deal of support by reaching out to other entrepreneurs, young and old. I would write to people that I admired and ask how they made it. To my surprise, they would write back. I would read and research constantly. I found inspiration from others success and failures. There is always something to learn.

The most important thing I did to make the business successful was to learn fast and solve problems quickly. As roadblocks developed I was able to try something new and see if it would work as a solution. For example, when we submitted our first design to the patent attorney for review he said our concept was unlikely to be patentable. He explained that our design was too similar to an existing patent and that we would have to redesign some features. With about one hour worth of drawing we were able to modify the product and clear the hurdle. Giving up was not an option and I knew that I would just have to work at the problem to come up with a better option than when we started. If I had been rigid in my thinking I never would have gotten the business off the ground.

This trait has served me well on numerous occasions. When brain storming with my parents one night early in the life of the business, we were thinking about how we would attract people to the product. We knew there were people out there who were interested in fruit infused water but we had to find a way to reach them. We knew we had to have an answer to this problem if the business was to be financially viable. At the time, there was only one web site devoted to the concept and it had little in the way of content. We set out to create the highest ranking fruit infused water recipe web site on a Google search and were able to achieve this within 2 months. Using Google analytics, we were able to determine what was attracting people to our site. Learning very quickly about what was working and what did not allowed us to focus our energy on the things that were generating the most user engagement. We had to quickly adapt our model as we learned what was successful and move those concepts to the front of our plan. It was through this web site that we caught the eye of the William J. Clinton Foundation and led to our biggest promotional success to date. They invited our family to attend the prestigious Health Matters conference and initiated our affiliation with the Alliance for a Healthier Generation. I learned the trait of quickly adapting to situations from watching my mother at work. In her role as a business development consultant, I saw her actively troubleshoot problems and learn how to respond to roadblocks.

Initially, I became frustrated when concepts did not pan out, but I learned to pivot quickly as the project progressed. For instance, I really wanted to make the base piece of our bottle out of stainless steel. I thought it would look really cool, but as the project developed we realized that it would be really cold if that re-freezable base piece ever touched someone's skin. So we made a quick adjustment and went with a different material. We never strayed from our guiding principles of making a product that improves health through fruit infused water, but we definitely did not take a straight path to get to our objective.

The concept of learning rapidly and adjusting to the situation is essential to someone starting a new business. Regardless of the type of business involved, there will be problems that come up and decisions that need to be made. However, it is not always clear what is the best answer and sometimes you just have to try an idea to see if it will work. When it didn't work out for me I found another way and tried again. I had to be flexible to reach my goal of getting a product to market, but I am passionate about my mission and determined to find a way to improve the health of my generation. This model will work for anyone building a new business. Learn quickly about what is working, be flexible with your concepts, and constantly move forward towards your goal.

Also, keep an eye on the amount of money needed to keep the business afloat. Raising capital is important for any new venture and early on I recognized I needed to identify how much cash we would need for the first year. Early in the creation of the business we tried to forecast what we would need to get through our first production run. I raised capital through crowd-funding to help contribute to the costs of production and my parents contributed the rest. Thus far any money that has been earned through crowd-funding is being reinvested in to the business. Our goal is to continue to reinvest monies earned back in to the business to expand our product line, however, we have also agreed to donate a percent of our profits to the Alliance for a Healthier Generation in support of their goals of reducing childhood obesity.

» **What is the most important advice you would give to other entrepreneurs?**

Being an entrepreneur is exciting and an emotional experience. It takes a great deal of perseverance, confidence, and dedication. I have learned a tremendous amount about business in the last 10 months and the hands on experience is far better than anything I have learned from a book. I am looking forward to the next stages in building the business and moving from a start-up to a multi-product company.

www.definebottle.com

@definebottle

www.facebook.com/definebottle

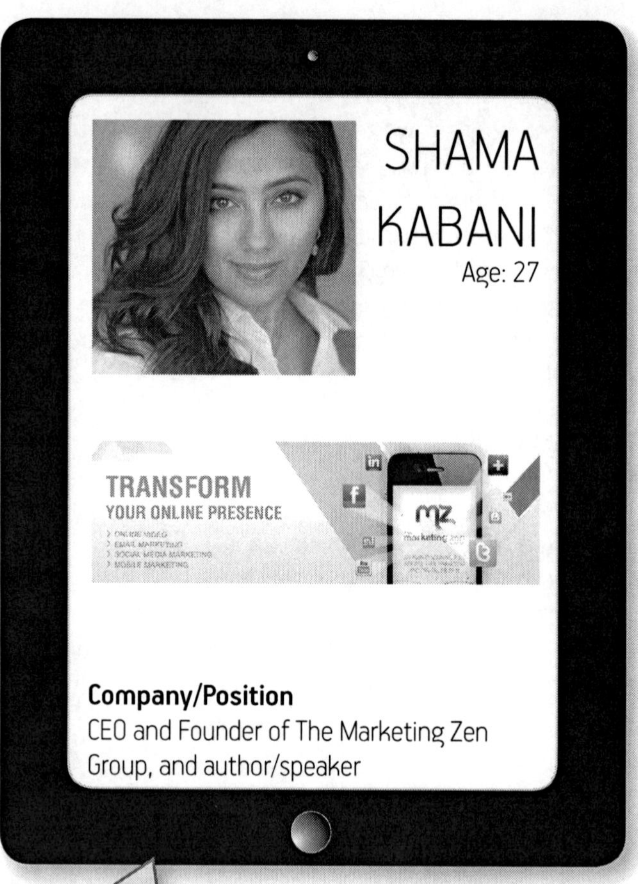

Shama Kabani is a technology entrepreneur, a best-selling author, a public speaker, and a web and television personality. ***Marketing Zen*** is an award winning online ***marketing*** company with proven results providing services in SEO, web design and development, and social media. The Marketing Zen Group is a full-service online marketing and digital PR firm dedicated to providing strategy and implementation services for businesses, organizations, and non-profits looking to fully leverage the internet.

» **Give a detailed description of the work that you do. What are your job responsibilities?**

There is no typical day, but I enjoy that. Some days, I speak in a different city or country. Other days, I am in the studio shooting various media segments. Every day, regardless of my location, I work with the team at The Marketing Zen Group. Since we are a virtual company, my location doesn't deter me from joining in.

» **What made you think of your idea?**

I studied social media in graduate school. This was when Twitter had 2,000 users, not the 200 million that it has today. Upon graduation, I realized that social media had huge implications for the business world. The corporate world just wasn't ready to hear it at that time, so I started The Marketing Zen Group. Within 2 years, we went from just me to 25 people. Today, we serve as a full service web marketing firm that works with companies around the world.

» **How did you get started?**

I started my own company, first doing social media consulting and then morphing into a full service online marketing firm. Today, we have 30 full-timers and a global clientele. We grew 425% alone in the past year.

» **What were the biggest challenges that you encountered?**

» **How did you get into this job? How easy or difficult it was for you to venture into this business?**

By fostering a very open environment. A business is only as good as the people behind it. We invest in our people, and then I make it a point to listen. I don't believe in motivating people. I believe in finding motivated people and allowing them space and resources to use that motivation. I am always excited at how creative the team can get.

» **Have you always been interested in this kind of work?**

Growing up, I wanted to do multiple things. I wanted to be a journalist, a teacher, and I even toyed with the idea of Bollywood! My mom is an actress, so she was very supportive. My dad wanted me to be a doctor. What I do today is a combination of journalism, technology and media. I am very lucky that I have a career which combines all three which I am passionate about.

» **Where and how do you see yourself five or ten years from now?**

I plan to continue sharing my passion for technology with a broader audience via TV and the Web. How about two big visions? I am building two things right now. One is my company, The Marketing Zen Group. And I have plans to continue to grow the company. So, that's my CEO/Founder hat. The other hat is my TV/media career hat. I currently host a web TV show (Shama.Tv), as well as multiple segments on technology and business on TV (Tech Zen with Shama on CW 33 for example). I ***love*** making business and technology come alive for people. My team calls me the Rachael Ray of Tech, because I don't believe you have to be a geek or a nerd to "get technology" or to start a business. Anyone can do it if they have the will and willingness to learn.

» **What is the most important advice you would give to other entrepreneurs?**

The best advice is to listen to your marketplace. Truly listen to their needs, and then deliver on that. As we were growing, we noticed that we'd consult with clients on how to build a good website for example. And then they would struggle to find the designers and developers that also understood the vision like us. We had a lot of clients saying – why don't you just do it all for us? This is why we became a full service web marketing & PR company. It was scary because it required more resources, but you have to learn to listen to your clients. Especially when you are in the bootstrapping phase.

www.marketingzen.com

@ Shama

www.facebook.com/marketingzengroup

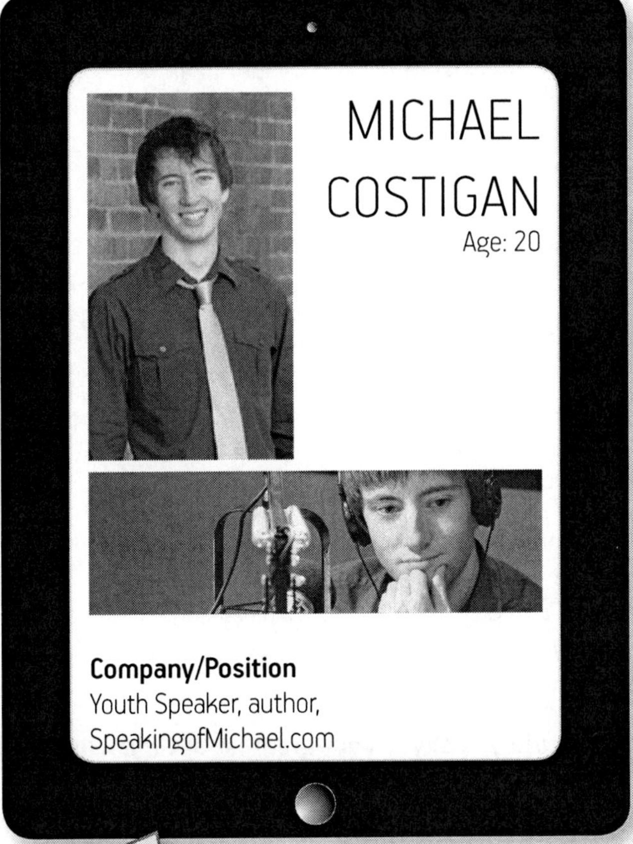

An internationally recognized speaker, Michael has earned a reputation as a leading authority on youth leadership. He helps teens find their passion and discover their future. Michael has been featured on networks such as FOX, ABC, CBS and NPR.

» **Give a detailed description of the work that you do. What are your job responsibilities?**

I speak to students primarily in high school and colleges across the country. My message is aimed at helping them find their passion and discover their future. A big part of my job is crafting an entertaining, inspiring, and empowering speech that is uniquely tailored to each audience I visit. The job means I must travel a great deal, from schools to conferences all over the US and even in other countries. It's an extremely rewarding 'job', so much so that I don't consider it one at all.

» **What made you think of your idea?**

After having opportunities to speak at high schools as a result of early business ventures I had when I was younger, I met a fellow speaker by the name of Josh Shipp. He encouraged me and taught me almost everything I know about the speaking world today.

» **What were the biggest challenges that you encountered?**

Initially it was challenging to settle on the message that I have now because I wasn't sure how audiences would react, whether or not it was a compelling story, and whether or not event planners would book the message I could offer.

» **What would you say is your greatest accomplishment along on the way?**

In 2012 I flew to Saudi Arabia to keynote the 2nd Annual Young Leader's Gulf Forum. This was perhaps the biggest honor I have received as a young speaker.

» **What is the most challenging part of your job and why?**

One of the most challenging aspects of my job is ensuring that I am always offering advice and knowledge to my audience that they can act on and benefit from. We've all heard speakers that we felt didn't teach us anything new or motivate us to change things in our lives. I go through a great deal of effort to be better than that and really want to get to know my audience before every engagement.

» **What do you think helped you the most in your success?**

I've sought out the advice of the top dozen or so Youth Speakers in my field. Collectively, all of these speakers helped me shape my message, brand, and business. A few notable shout outs go to Josh Shipp, Brooks Gibbs, Ryan Porter, and Grant Baldwin.

» **Where and how do you see yourself five or ten years from now?**

10 Years from now I hope to have a platform where I can reach my audience at any time through social media, mainstream media, and events that my brand puts on for people from around the world.

» **What is the most important advice you would give to other entrepreneurs?**

Many people think the surest way to success and happiness is conformity. They're wrong. When you're young you have the chance to take chances, to risk it all, and to only gain from your experiences.

 www.speakingofmichael.com

 @michaelcostigan

 www.facebook.com/MichaelCostigan

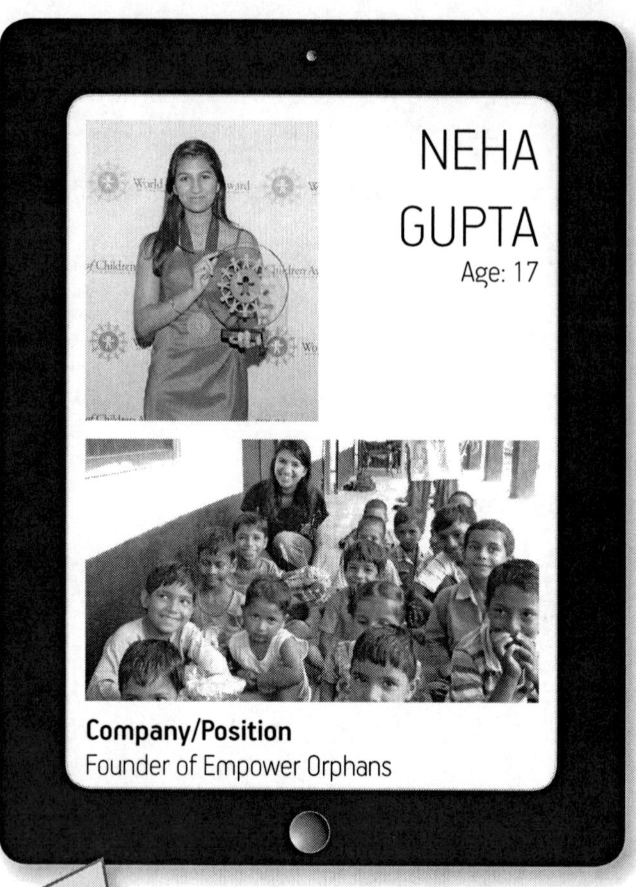

Neha Gupta is a bright young entrepreneur aiming to change the world. Neha empowers disadvantaged and orphaned children in India with basic literacy and technology skills to prepare them for the future. Empower Orphans is a non-profit organization which intends to address the problems associated with orphans and abandoned children, and children born into homes living in poverty. The organization's goal is to help create self-sufficiency by supplying children with the tools to gain a basic education and technical skills to enable a sustainable livelihood. In addition to education, Empower Orphans provides food, clothing, health care, and medical supplies to establish an effective learning environment.

» **The problem:**

According to the United Nations there are approximately 145 million abandoned children in the world with the majority being orphans. Unless these children are adopted or absorbed by an institution, they are left to wander the streets, beg or steal food, and find shelter wherever they can. These children are helpless and frequent victims of violence, sexual exploitation and disease. Without the support from their families, these children often turn to organized crime and prostitution for survival – frequently resulting in early death and a perpetuation of a vicious cycle. In India, 42% of the population lives below the international poverty line (earning less than $1.25 per day). Children born to these households have little if any access to education. At best, their school attendance is sporadic, as the family lacks the funds to regularly pay school fees. Further, these children are often required to mind younger siblings or required to earn money.

» **How did you get started?**

As my grandparents live in India, I visit the country every year. In keeping with family tradition, I volunteer at an orphanage along with my parents each time we visit my grandparents' hometown located in northern India. When I was nine years old, I realized that the 200 children who lived at the orphanage did not have the means gain even a basic education. I felt very sad when I heard this because I know education is very important. Moreover, it was heartbreaking for me to think that these children had no parent to guide them, protect them, or love them. Instead of internalizing these feelings and merely showing empathy for the orphans, I decided to take action by raising money to facilitate their education. On returning home to the United States, I held a garage sale and raised money to buy books for the orphans by selling my toys. Over the years, through multiple fundraising events my organization has distributed goods and services in excess of $1 million dollars and has positively impacted the livesof25,000children.

I firmly believe that every child has the right to hope. This is why I founded Empower Orphans, a 501 (c) 3 non-profit organization when I was nine years old. My objective was to create self sufficiency among orphaned, abused and under privileged children through education and healthcare, enabling them to break the cycle of poverty and become productive members of society.

Although Empower Orphans started with the goal of helping orphans in India, we have expanded our activities to support:

Orphaned children in the United States

Underprivileged children (India and the United States) – The parents of these children are predominantly maids and manual laborers and the majority live at or below the poverty line. They are unable to afford regular education or healthcare for their children.

Lower caste children (India) – The majority of families living under the poverty line belong to the lower castes – an evil still in prevalence. Given society strictures, children born to these families have little if any means of gaining an education and breaking the cycle of poverty. Empower Orphans has leveraged its influence in gaining admission for these children into schools and sponsoring their education.

Critically at-risk girls (India) – To mitigate the risk of critically at-risk girls entering into prostitution to support themselves, Empower Orphans provides them with technical skills (sewing, tailoring) and supply several of them with sewing machines enabling them to start their own small businesses.

Sexually abused children (USA) – We provide small comforts to these children while they go through the judicial/criminal process.

» **The Impact**

Empower Orphans has distributed goods and services valued at more than $1,000,000 and has directly impacted the lives of over 25,000 orphaned and disadvantaged children in India and USA. Key highlights of accomplishments include:

» **EDUCATION:**

- Established 5 libraries at 2 orphanages and 3 disadvantaged schools located in India and the United States.
- Founded 4 computer labs at disadvantaged school in India and US. The labs have a total of 18 computers, printers, power backup and internet facilities).
- Established a sewing center with 60 sewing machines (Impact: 2000 older girls ages 17-21).
- Sponsored the complete education (up to graduation) of 100 disadvantaged children
- A science center was also set up at a school for disadvantaged children

» **HEALTHCARE**

- Furnished apartments for hundreds of underprivileged families living within Bucks County, PA by providing 100 van loads of home furnishings. Further, Empower Orphans has provided diapers for over 5,000 children. Empower Orphans partners with a local hospital outreach program to activate this program.

- Installed a water well and a water purification system in a village in India

- Conducted a 4 day Eye and Dental Clinic for 360 under privileged children in India. The doctors evaluated the needs of each child and advanced treatment was provided to the children as appropriate. 56 children were provided additional eye care and 103 children with extensive dental treatment.

- Provided nutritious meals, school books, school bags, footwear, warm clothes and blankets to thousands of children.

I strongly believe in investing in the future by learning the appropriate skills. I relate the story of Meena to illustrate my point. I met Meena when she was 18 years old. She lived in a small village in Northern India. Her home consisted of a single room which was shared by six people. Meena's father had lost his job and the family had no income. Meena came to the sewing center set up by Empower Orphans to learn the skills necessary of a seamstress. On her graduation, she was given a sewing machine to enable her to start her own business. Meena began earning money and used it to bring electricity into her house for the first time – one light bulb suspended by a wire. Having light in the house enabled her brother, Ram to study at night and pass an electrician's qualifying exam. Now, Ram too, is earning a living and both he and Meena support their family. This was possible because of ONE sewing machine that cost only $40. Knowing that I had been able to make a vast difference in someone's life gave me tremendous satisfaction. Changing a life is incomparable to any other experience that you will ever have. Seeing someone else smile and knowing that you put that smile on their face, and knowing that they wake up every morning because of you, is a wonderful feeling. You will never forget it, and as long as you live.

» **Where and how do you see yourself five or ten years from now?**

In the future I plan to continue my social and community activities by opening additional libraries, computer centers, and trade schools. These schools will enable the children to learn a trade, facilitating them to earn a living and become productive members of society.

» **About me**

I am a senior at Pennsbury High School in Yardley, Pennsylvania. Other than my focus on my organization (Empower Orphans), I am active in the school community. I am on the Board for the School District and on the high school tennis team.

» **What are your greatest accomplishments?**

My proudest moment (and probably more so for my parents as they are first generation immigrants) was when the US Congress raised a US flag over the US Capitol in Washington, D.C. to honor my services to the community. I was also invited to the White House to participate in a strategy session on youth volunteerism.

» **What is the most important advice you would give to other entrepreneurs?**

There are countless problems that we face in the world today and each and every person in this world has the power to change society. History has proven it, and I have realized that age does not matter. The movement of change does not require a lot of people; just one person can achieve change. It simply takes determination and perseverance to turn empathy into action, and once you do, you will see just how rewarding your efforts will be. One person truly has the power to change society if he/she converts empathy into action.

www.empowerorphans.org

@_EmpowerOrphans

www.facebook.com/pages/Empower-Orphans/173363152721734

Juliette founded MissOandFriends.com at fifteen years old, and is now the head of the multi-million-dollar company. ***Miss O & Friends*** is a safe online site for girls to play cool free games fashion dress up games, makeover games, word games, enter free online contests, and much more.

» **Give a detailed description of the work that you do. What are your job responsibilities?**

As a co-founder, I do a bunch of different things for Miss O. My main responsibilities are bringing in sponsorships for different tween girl products. We work a lot with publishing companies so I'm always figuring out creative ways to integrate different products into the site, which encourage interaction amongst our users. I'm also the spokesperson for the company so I talk to the press, do interviews and promote Miss O in any way that I can. I also am involved in the creative side of Miss O from web design to conceptual product ideas. I also work on the back end of the website in the admin updating content. There is a column on Miss O & Friends called "Just from Juliette" and I provide advice to girls based on my experiences as a tween and my friends. My job responsibilities are a good combo between creative and managerial, which is great that I get to do both.

» **What made you think of your idea?**

Miss O & Friends was inspired by drawings that I did when I was 10. I was with my family coming back from vacation when I started drawing these girls that I called 'Cool Girls.' My mom, Hermine, is a graphic designer so she took my drawings and transferred them onto the computer. My younger sister, Olivia (who is the real 'Miss O') also got involved and for a while it was pretty much just a hobby for my mom, sister and I. When Olivia turned 8, my parents had a birthday party for her where my made 'Miss O-like' characters for my sisters friends. She blew them up really big and mounted them so when the girls walked into our house, they saw characters that looked like them. They went crazy for them and kept talking about how much they loved them. I was 13 at the time and still in middle school, while Olivia was 8 and was going to be entering middle school in a few years. Middle school is a really difficult time for young girls with so many new things going on; their bodies changing, cliques, boys, bullying, school work, parents, etc., and I wanted to create something for my sister and her friends to help them through these difficult years since there wasn't anything like Miss O that existed. With the help of my parents, my mom being a graphic designer and my dad, Paul, having a background in business, I was able to start the company in April 2005.

» **How did you get started?**

There was really no business in mind when we first started, so it has been really cool how it has been able to grow. When Miss O first started the website was super simple. There was a homepage, which had the five Miss O girls and simple flash animations. There was hardly anything to it, but it was definitely a start. With the input of so many tween girls, we were able to start to develop the site in a way that would attract our target audience. If you look at the site now, you can see how much it has grown and expanded since our simple flash homepage. The company has transformed a great deal. We started off with a business plan that we have used as our guide, but that business plan is always changing. We find new ways to engage girls, to generate revenue and new outlets and channels that are appropriate for Miss O and our community.

» **What were the biggest challenges that you encountered?**

There are a lot of challenging parts, when things get hard or when something turns out the way you didn't expect it to keep going and moving forward. There are always setbacks and there's always hard stuff that is going to happen so just realizing that day was that day and keep moving forward. Our servers crash or there's a hacker or something happens with the site and it's all chaotic. Especially with working with a website is always constant monitoring and its always making sure everything is safe, and making sure were keeping the privacy of everyone, and creating content that is good. The biggest stress is always when something happens with the server and our site is down. It's always dramatic.

» **What was it like when you realized you made your first million?**

It's always a process. It's always really exiting. We work really hard, and it's exciting and great, and I just want to keep going!

» **What important lessons have you learned in the process of establishing your company?**

There are a bunch of important lessons I have learned. The most important lesson that I have learned is to work with other people and to partner with other people who believe in your idea and who see potential and who also posses the passion you process for whatever your company is whatever your brand is. Because if your just working with someone who doesn't truly believe in it, they're not going to put there all into it and it's not going to work out for anyone. When you start a company you are the last person to get paid. So having people around you and working with people who are able to sacrifice their time, take their time put in their effort, for something that everyone is really passionate about is really important.

» **What do you think helped you the most in your success?**

There are a lot of things that have helped me. I work with my family so my parents have always been such a huge support of all of this, they saw potential in my idea and they put a lot of their own money behind it, which there would be no miss o and friends without their involvement. My parents being so supportive and really believing in the idea has really contributed to the success.

» **Where and how do you see yourself five or ten years from now?**

I have no idea. In the short term I just want to continue to grow Miss O and friends into the brand that it is.

» **What is the most important advice you would give to other entrepreneurs?**

When you're starting out and you have an idea something important to realize is you can't always do it alone, some people can do it alone, but it is really important to find a team to find people you trust and to find people who you can work well with and can help you and again believe in your idea and are really passionate about it. You yourself have to be really passionate about it. You don't want to just start a business just to start a business. It has to be something that you believe in and you're willing to dedicate a lot of time to and really have it take over your life for a fair amount of time because Success doesn't happen overnight, and when it does it is a rare case. It's always process. Being an entrepreneur the biggest thing I would say to aspiring entrepreneurs is to know that it's a process and to know that it doesn't happen overnight and it really does take a lot of hard work a lot of time and that it's not easy.

www.missoandfriends.com

@JulietteBrindak

www.facebook.com/MissOandFriends

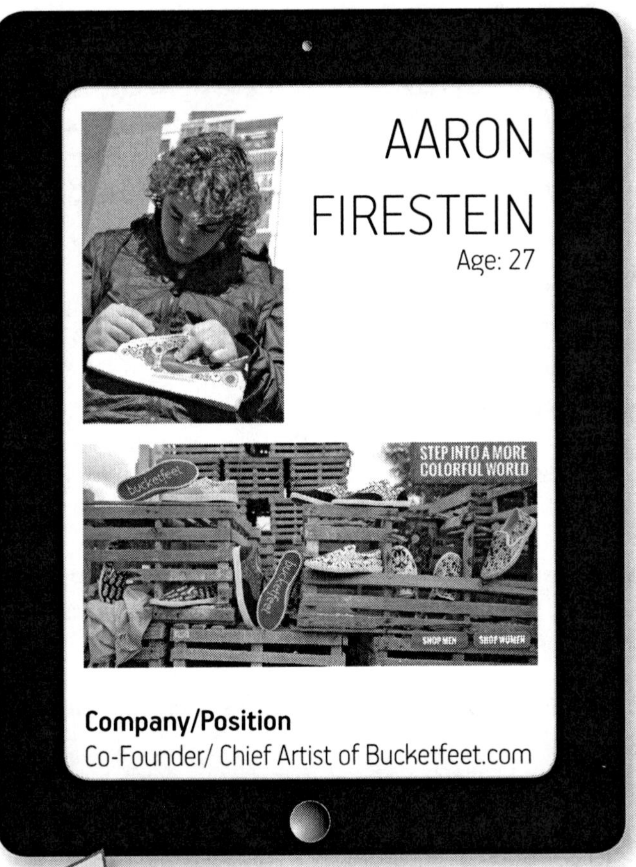

Aaron is a talented artistic entrepreneur. Creating a job that he could apply his artistic abilities to, Aaron started a company that is not only successful, but very cool. BucketFeet is artist designed footwear. We give artists a platform to share their stories and showcase their art. Step into a more colorful world with unique, comfortable shoes that stand out from the crowd. Each shoe is the result of a carefully crafted vision and handmade design. We value creative art and passionate individuals. Every person is different and so is every shoe. This means you get a product that is as individual and original as you are. And when people ask you about your shoes, and they will, you'll have a great story to tell.

» **Give a detailed description of the work that you do. What are your job responsibilities?**

I am one of the co-Founders and the Chief Artist. We all wear a lot of hats when it comes to roles and responsibilities, but my most important role is to be the point person between the company and all the talented artists we work with. This means initiating conversations all the way to product design. I also do sales-related stuff, blogging, social media, etc...

» **What made you think of your idea?**

I bought a white pair of Vans back in 2007 and decided to draw on them. The rest is history!

» **How did you get started?**

Like I mentioned, I was bored with the white Vans I had so I decided to customize them. People loved what I created and bit by bit, starting selling them. It all started with me drawing on shoes.

» **What were the biggest challenges that you encountered?**

Money is always a big concern when you start a business. That was definitely the biggest thing at the beginning.

» **What would you say is your greatest accomplishment along on the way?**

I think raising capital and hiring a team is our biggest accomplishment to date. We have a solid crew here and we're able to do a lot more with more hands on deck than we were before.

» **Have you always been interested in this kind of work?**

I always knew I wouldn't work a normal 9-5 office job, that's for sure. I also knew I'd likely work in some sort of creative field, just didn't know it was going to be shoes.

» **What is the most challenging part of your job and why?**

I think always trying to stay ahead of the game and trying to stay creative is challenging. I put a lot of pressure on myself but I try to enjoy it as much as I can.

» **What fulfillment do you get from your job?**

I'm following a dream.

» **What important lessons have you learned in the process of establishing your company?**

Hire good people, don't take your foot off the gas pedal, and do the best you can!

» **Where and how do you see yourself five or ten years from now?**

Hopefully we'll still be a relevant company and will be THE brand for artist-designed footwear. I hope to continue to be a part of something special - hopefully will be working from a beach somewhere though.

» **What is the most important advice you would give to other entrepreneurs?**

Don't be afraid to fail. Most great lessons come from failure.

 www.bucketfeet.com

 @AaronFuegostein

 www.facebook.com/bucketfeet

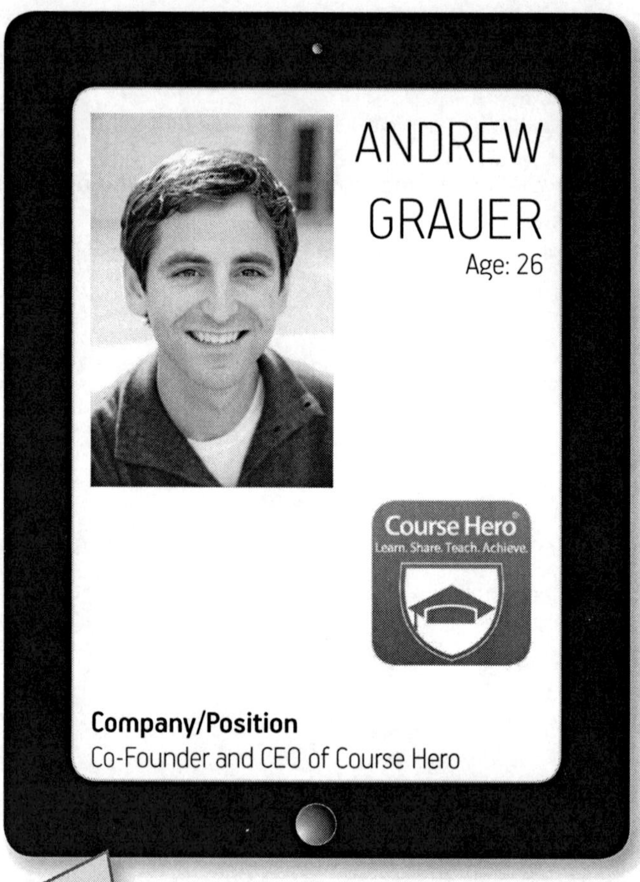

While in college Andrew came up with a plan to help students that miss class or need notes easily get what they need. Andrew has always had an entrepreneurial spirit and that is how he came up with his business. Course Hero is an online learning platform for students to access study resources like course materials, flashcards, educational videos and tutors. Its educator portal is a micropublishing platform for educators to distribute their educational resources. Course Hero collects and organizes study materials like practice exams, problem sets, syllabi, flashcards, class notes and study guides from users who upload. Users either buy a subscription or upload documents in order to receive membership and access website material. ***CourseHero*** is an online platform providing educational resources to help students learn more effectively.

» **Give a detailed description of the work that you do. What are your job responsibilities?**

I run and manage Course Hero, an online learning platform that provides a suite of digital education resources including free, curated courses, online tutoring service, digital flashcards and crowd-sourced study materials. My job responsibilities consist of approving and overseeing all activity within the business, in addition to meeting with education players throughout the industry including teachers, students, university executives, content creators, media and other edtech founders to inform the future direction of the company.

» **What made you think of your idea?**

I founded Course Hero while I was a student at Cornell University because I was frustrated that so much knowledge was bottled up in private hard drives and individual brains without a convenient, accessible forum to share and distribute this knowledge. So, I took a semester off from school and founded Course Hero with my brothers David and Jared to create a better learning experience – one that benefits both the learner and the subject matter expert.

» **How did you get started?**

My brothers and I began our journey by pooling $10,000 of our own money. Given that we were in school, this was a meaningful amount of money, so we made it last. We eventually turned to our parents to raise over $100,000 when we had more confidence in the company's prospects.

» **What were the biggest challenges that you encountered?**

The edtech industry is really only just beginning. This is both exciting and challenging because there is no real model to follow. This leaves a lot of room for experimentation to find out what is most effective.

» **What would you say is your greatest accomplishment along on the way?**

Not giving up along the way.

» **How did you get into this job? How easy or difficult it was for you to venture into this business?**

I created the job by co-founding the company with my brothers. It's never easy to create your own business, but education is something I'm passionate about, which made starting the business worth all the hard work.

» **Have you always been interested in this kind of work?**

I love strategy games and building things. The idea of starting with limited resources and competing to build things in a competitive environment with multiple players is a huge passion of mine.

» **What has this experience been like? Any interesting points you would like to share?**

The experience has been very satisfying but not always enjoyable. I wouldn't want to be doing anything else, and I feel so lucky to be able to do what I do. That said, there is an incredible amount of stress involved in this rollercoaster path of entrepreneurship. Mark Suster says it well here what you have to deal with: http://techcrunch.com/2011/01/30/should-you-really-be-a-startup-entrepreneur/

» **What is the most challenging part of your job and why?**

Focus and prioritization: Focus on doing things that align directly with our core strategy and not spending time and resources on other things than that. I have to be a supreme editor and help other leads do the same.

» **What fulfillment do you get from your job?**

Learning is, of course, important from an altruistic point of view, but I'm really excited about the steps we're taking to make the learning system more sustainable. You hear a lot about the inequity in the current education system. Teachers feel like they're not getting paid enough for doing their job and with tuition continually increasing, students feel like they're paying too much for their education. It's great to know we're providing a 24/7 service that is helping students learn new subjects matters and/or providing them the tools to help them execute better in the courses they're already taking. In addition, we're giving educators and experts a platform for them to share (and monetize) their knowledge. It's great to be able to provide experts with more opportunities and students with the access to resources to help them learn more efficiently.

» **What was it like when you realized you made your first million?**

It's still all illiquid paper money. So, that's one thing. I can't actually use it or be distracted by it. At the same time, I think the realization that I could have millions of dollars allowed me to realize that money isn't my top priority. My life wouldn't be much different with many more millions of dollars. It's allowed me to focus most on creating value, helping others create value, be passionate, and focus on how to create happiness in my life and others'.

» **What important lessons have you learned in the process of establishing your company?**

You can rev on ideas all day long and it takes a certain type of person to just start acting and keep going with an idea. In the end, being an entrepreneur is not just about having an idea – it's about having the initiative to go out there and make an idea happen.

» **What do you think helped you the most in your success?**

Support from my friends and family was a huge factor in my success. Without their support I wouldn't be where I am today. It's important to have a strong support system that is there for you in the ups and downs that come with starting a business.

In addition, I really valued what I learned in Cornell's entrepreneurship program. Not only was I able to take courses, but I also had the opportunity to talk to key faculty in the program. I got great advice and mentorship from John Jaquette and I've carried that relationship with me after I graduated and as I continue to move forward with Course Hero.'

» **Where and how do you see yourself five or ten years from now?**

I see myself helping Course Hero become a huge marketplace and community for digital learning.

» **How do you spend money – business or personal-wise?**

Because initial funding came from my personal bank account and family support, I was motivated to make Course Hero a sustainable business that wasn't dependent on outside dollars, so we could be in the position to take more risks. Unlike many other players in the space, Course Hero has been profitable for a number of years. Since the online education market is in its infancy, having this liquidity has allowed us to experiment to find out which educational models and approaches will work best with our student base.

» **What is the most important advice you would give to other entrepreneurs?**

One thing I've seen from other young start-ups is the feeling that they need to give away a lot of equity in the beginning. I worry that this dilutes the business too much early on. Having other funding, whether that comes from personal savings or from friends and family, allows businesses to get things started on much fairer terms.

www.coursehero.com

@atgrauer

www.facebook.com/coursehero

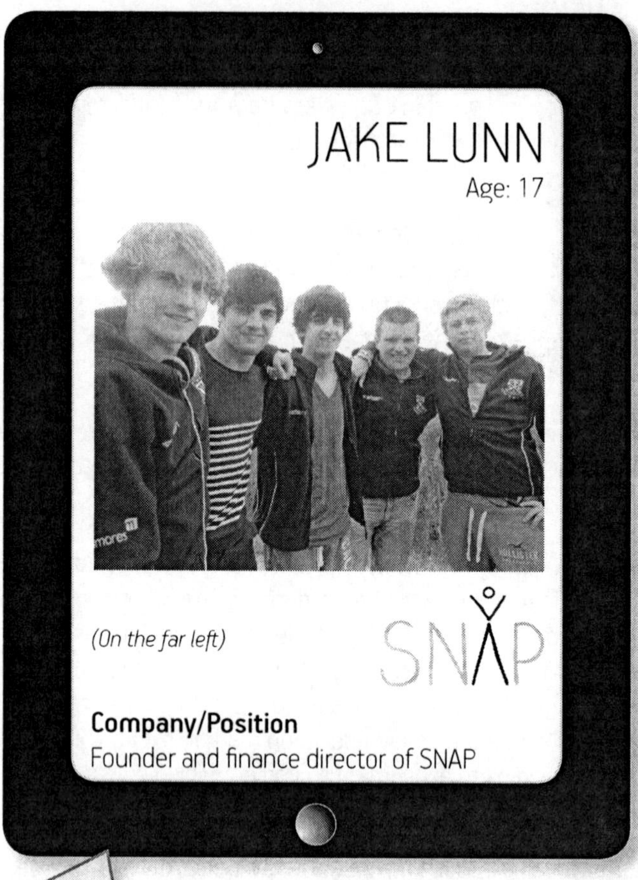

Jakes first company was started at age 11. Jake had such a passion for boats that he created a company that made custom napkins to be used on ships and yachts. SNAP is not just another online planner. It saves everyone time and simplifies the homework planning and monitoring process for teachers, students and parents using the latest mobile technology, as well as still being accessible via a computer. Teachers tell us that the homework brief written in planners by students is often incomplete, rushed and not always understood by everyone. How many times do students come home and find they don't fully understand their own notes. Teachers love SNAP and they write the brief that can be looked up, "no more excuses". Parents tell us that they would love to have equal access to the homework brief, so that they too can keep an eye on their child's progress and help them plan their time. They don't really want to wait until the school report to find out that homework has not always been on time. They have told us that they love the idea of SNAP as it makes them involved.

» **Give a detailed description of the work that you do. What are your job responsibilities?**

Ok so I'm 17, currently working as finance director for a company I helped set up called SNAP. It is run entirely by people my age. Personally I work very closely with the managing director to run the company. The ownership of the company is spread throughout the group. SNAP stands for School Networking Application Platform and is basically an online planner for teachers parents and students. The idea is that is it incredibly easy to use at a very affordable price and solves many problems for the users. Myself and the managing director share the roles of organizing the team of 20 working with us. I arrange sales meeting with schools and then go out to these schools to pitch to them. Recently we took our product to The Education Show in Birmingham which required a lot of organizing followed by a lot of follow up work. Then of course as my title suggests, I control all of the money in the business. This is one of the easier jobs!

» **What made you think of your idea?**

It started as a Young Enterprise competition. The idea came from the group of us that volunteered sitting in a room and coming up with as many problems as we could. This wasn't just targeted at schools, this was problems for everyone. We eventually found a whole load of problems in homework setting. It takes time, rarely gets done and parents hardly ever know what homework their child has. We then came up with a solution to this using the resources we had (two software engineers in the group).

» **What is the most challenging part of your job and why?**

Our biggest challenge was our first sale. Although we are yet to meet someone who doesn't like the idea of our product, it is very hard to convince anyone that untested technology worked. We spent hours preparing the pitch that we used for the school most likely to trust us- our own. Once we sold it once and had proof that the system worked it was much easier to sell.

» **What has been your greatest accomplishment along the way?**

The greatest accomplishment has to therefore be overcoming the challenge of the first sale. That gave us the money to take our product to The Education Show and without that our company would not be where it is now.

» **How did you get started?**

Getting into this job was easy. I have very little technical ability, I can just about use my computer and that is it, writing software was never an area I saw myself in. However it is all about taking opportunities and although it is not my personal area of strength it is an area I enjoy working in.

» **What fulfillment do you get from your job?**

The whole experience is fantastic! I love the challenges and I love the feeling of overcoming the challenges and making the business profitable.

» **How do you spend money – business or personal-wise?**

I spend my money on the things I love doing. My hobbies are probably my main drive for making money. I have an extremely expensive taste in sports. I like kitesurfing, surfing, snowboard, skiing and wake boarding. I also love to travel and when I can combine the two! This is an expensive lifestyle to lead for a 17 year old!

» **What do you think helped you the most in your success?**

I would not consider myself successful just yet. I am aiming for success, and that being having enough money to lead the lifestyle I would like to lead, and therefore I am not there yet. However my parents are who help me the most. They run a business of their own and we regularly talk about it. Any tough decisions and I tend to ask for advice. Ten years time. I would like to be based on the east coast of Australia with the freedom to travel and do what I like without being tied down to a 9-5.

» **What is the most important advice you would give to other entrepreneurs?**

Advice, my main advice would be use what you have and who you have. You can never get too much help or advice. Learn from other peoples mistakes before making them yourself. Don't be afraid to make mistakes and most of all don't be afraid to try. Take whatever opportunities come your way, even if they are not 100% ideal for you, if it works out- awesome, if it doesn't-try again.

www.snapschool.co.uk

@jakelunn95

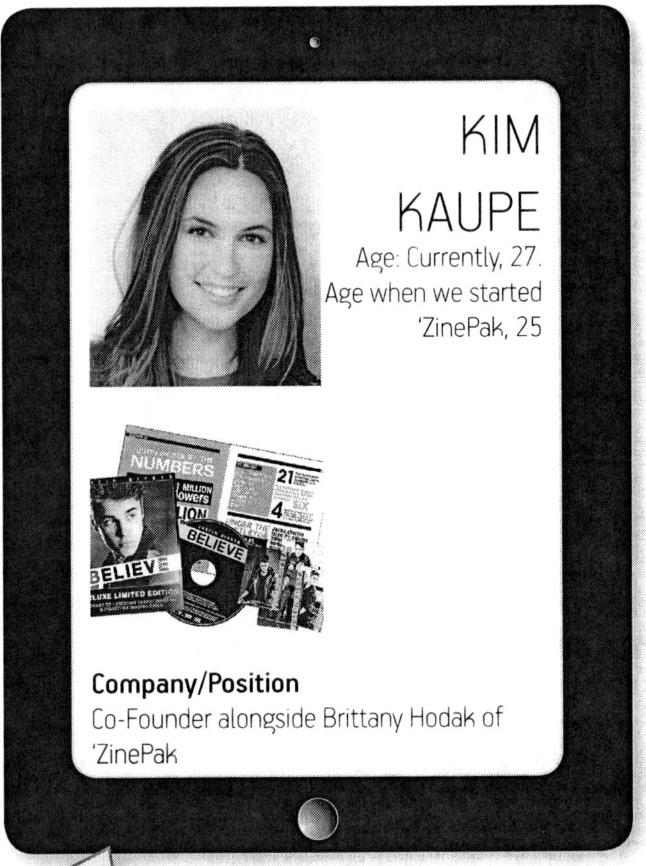

KIM KAUPE

Age: Currently, 27.
Age when we started 'ZinePak, 25

Company/Position
Co-Founder alongside Brittany Hodak of 'ZinePak

Kim is a creative and successful entrepreneur who was able to turn an idea into a reality. ZinePak was made of a combination of the things Kim and her co founder Brittany love, music and magazines. As huge fans of entertainment they created products that can excite and entertain almost anyone. That's ZEEN-pack, as in magazine package. The ZinePak configuration pairs a small-format magazine and exclusive, branded merchandise into one must-have package that's tailor made for super-fans. A ZinePak includes 64–120 pages of original content and a physical promotional item. Plus, every release is different because it's custom made, specifically for you. Whether you're a brand, artist, entertainment franchise, or athlete, a ZinePak can take your audience engagement to the next level.

» **Give a detailed description of the work that you do. What are your job responsibilities?**

'ZinePak (pronounced ZEEN-pack) creates custom publications paired with merchandise and media for fans. These engaging packages have been distributed everywhere from Walmart stores in the music section for new albums to out on tour with superstar artists. My job responsibilities vary everyday but the majority is spent brainstorming and coming up with new and dynamic ideas for the 'ZinePak configuration.

» **What made you think of your idea?**

My background is from the publishing industry and Brittany's is from the music industry. We paired our two ideas to create a mix of music, magazines, and fun that we thought fans would really enjoy!

» **How did you get started?**

We started in the company in January 2011 with an idea and a rough outline of a plan. We knew we wanted to reach passionate fans who wanted to learn more about their favorite recording artists. We used past industry contacts to garner interest from Walmart and major record labels. Our first year we completed 6 projects, however by the end of 2012 we grew 350% with 24 projects in a single year!

» **What were the biggest challenges that you encountered?**

We continue to face a range of challenges at 'ZinePak, everything from being taken seriously despite being young females in a male dominated industry to figuring out how to find the best computer software for our business. We, like many fellow entrepreneurs, have found solace in like-minded networking groups and organizations. Two that have helped us along the way are the Count Me In organization as well as Young Entrepreneurs Council.

» **What would you say is your greatest accomplishment along on the way?**

Our greatest accomplishment was passing the one million dollar mark in revenue. Only 1.8% of women owned businesses ever surpass that point. Being part of that 1.8% while we were under the age of 30 was very meaningful for us.

» **Have you always been interested in this kind of work?**

I have always had an interest in entertainment, marketing, and making people happy! The best complement I could ever receive is watching someone who has never seen a 'ZinePak before open one and experience it. Seeing their surprise and delight is an added reminded that the long hours, loads of emails, and late nights are all worth it.

» **What is the most challenging part of your job and why?**

Educating others. As an entrepreneur you are constantly educating others on what you do, why you do, and your passion. Some days it can feel like you have had the same conversation five times and each time you have to be just as energetic as ever before. It's challenging some days to muster that same energy over and over again.

» **What fulfillment do you get from your job?**

I feel fulfilled and happy to create something new every day and to make fans happy along the way. There is also something to be said to making a tangible product that I can point to and say, "I did that last month!"

» **What do you think helped you the most in your success?**

My ability to make meaningful connections with others is one of my strengths. The worst thing in business is having enemies or people you rub the wrong way as you don't know where those people will be in the future.

» **Where and how do you see yourself five or ten years from now?**

Happy, healthy, and hopefully somewhere warm in the winter!

» **What is the most important advice you would give to other entrepreneurs?**

Ask for forgiveness not permission. Push boundaries and dare to dream.

 www.zinepak.com

 @kimkaupe

 www.facebook.com/ZinePak

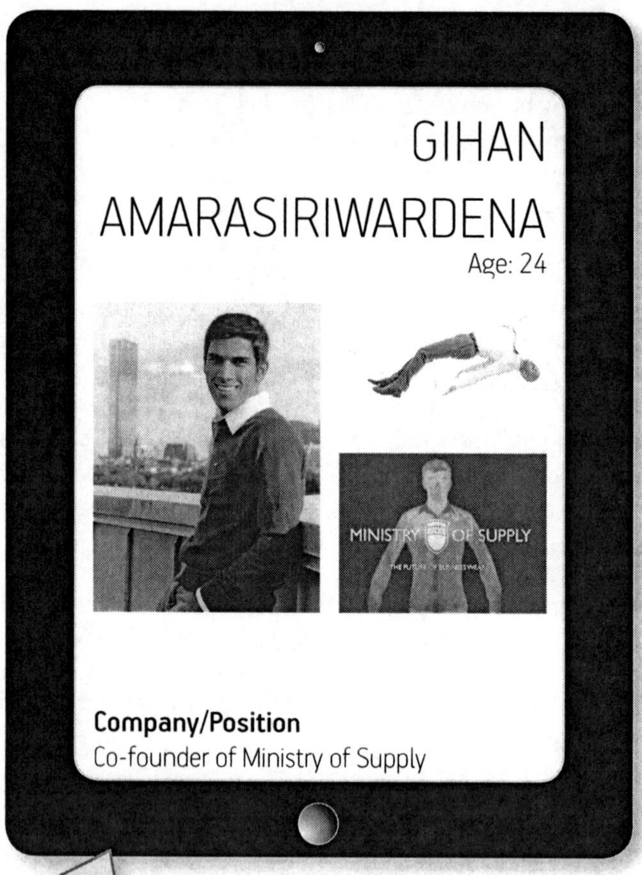

Gihan started Ministry of Supply with some classmates from MIT with the intention of creating technologically advanced office apparel. Passionate about performance apparel, Gihan began designing outdoor clothing as a Boy Scout when he was 14 and launched a small brand in high school based around materials he had developed. Gihan studied chemical-biological engineering at MIT and has always been a very smart and creative entrepreneur. Ministry of Supply is revolutionizing business apparel. While athletes have Under Armour, business attire has more or less stayed the same for the last century. Armed with some of the same technology NASA uses in its space suits, Ministry of Supply has developed a line of dress shirts called "Apollo" that adapt to your body to control perspiration, reduce odor, and make you feel like a million bucks.

» **Give a detailed description of the work that you do. What are your job responsibilities?**

I manage our Product Development and Creative Direction, in addition to some business development responsibilities

» **What made you think of your idea?**

I was a Boy Scout growing up and was passionate about outdoor clothing, and how performance materials allowed me to perform better. I designed climbing apparel in high school/college and did a lot of materials research in college. One of my friend's on the cross country team who worked in finance complained about how hot he'd get on the subway getting to work - we thought what if we took the materials from our running shirts and put them in business wear?

» **How did you get started?**

We started developing prototypes and a business plan during our senior spring semester. With no funding and only 3 prototypes, Kevin and I decided to turn down our full time job offers and work on MoS right after college. We spent 2011 developing our Dress shirt and base layer, and launched our first product in October 2011, over the next 6 months, we iterated the product and sold about 1000 shirts. We met Kit and Aman our two other co-founders at MIT's entrepreneurship center, who had very similar ideas and teamed up. We launched our premier product on Kickstarter last summer when things really took off.

» **What were the biggest challenges that you encountered?**

Creating a team and organizational structure that promotes innovation but has accountability.

» **What would you say is your greatest accomplishment along on the way?**

Launching our Apollo shirt on Kickstarter and becoming the most funded fashion project of all time (at the time) selling $429K worth of product and have nearly 3000 customers.

» **How did you get into this job? How easy or difficult it was for you to venture into this business?**

I've always been passionate about performance apparel and product design, I had started several businesses in high school / college and so I felt it was my calling. That said, it's certainly been difficult, and leading a startup forces you to grow up very quickly out of college.

» **Have you always been interested in this kind of work?**

Yes, I've been designing clothes since I was 14 and have been passionate about performance materials from an even younger age.

» **What fulfillment do you get from your job?**

I enjoy bringing the process of invention to clothing.

» **What important lessons have you learned in the process of establishing your company?**

Choose your team wisely. Think not only what they bring to the table in the short term, but in the long term as well. Value both passion and skills.

» **What do you think helped you the most in your success?**

Having an amazing community of mentors, both from previous work experiences and college as well as investors who are helping me grow as an entrepreneur. They aren't afraid to be candid with me and provide me constructive feedback.

» **Where and how do you see yourself five or ten years from now?**

I'll probably still be with MoS through my 20s, and afterwards, I hope to go to graduate school for engineering design.

» **How do you spend money – business or personal-wise?**

I'm fairly frugal, but I'll invest in items that provide long-term value or experiences that help me grow like travel. Business wise, I like to stay lean, but being discerning on where to invest - whether or not we can determine the ROI.

» **What is the most important advice you would give to other entrepreneurs?**

Surround yourself with people smarter than you - that's the best way to learn.

www.ministryofsupply.com

@ MinistrySupply

www.facebook.com/ministryofsupply

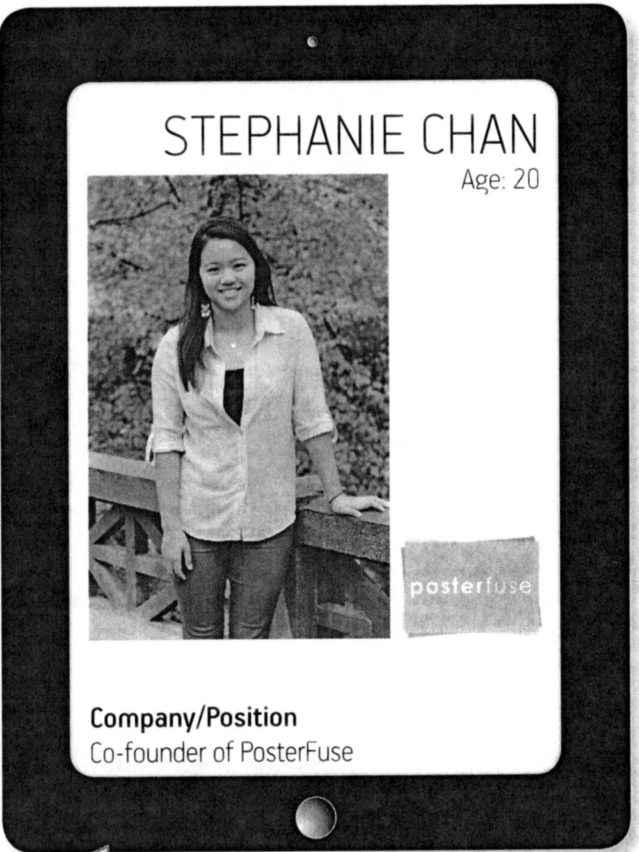

While in college Stephanie wanted to get creative with decorating her dorm room with something unique and cool. That is how Stepahnie got the idea to start her company called PosterFuse. PosterFuse takes the vast world of digital media that we are creating every day and transforms it into something tangible. PosterFuse allows users to access their Facebook and Instagram photos and easily drag and drop them onto a custom PosterFuse template. Users can even upload their own photos and add colors to their poster. What makes PosterFuse unique is how simple and intuitive it is to create an awesome customized poster.

» **Give a detailed description of the work that you do. What are your job responsibilities?**

I'm part of a 3 person team that runs PosterFuse - a web-platform that allows users to design a customized 20x32" poster of their Instagram and Facebook photos. My role entails strategy and execution for marketing, public relations and partnerships. On a day-to-day basis, I'm in contact with customers, potential parters and the press. I also write content and update our social media sites.

» **What made you think of your idea?**

I met my two co-founders through working on another project at Emory University and we soon learnt we had similar passions, interests and that together we would make a great team. After tossing around ideas and getting feedback, we were having lunch and needed to figure out a way to decorate our rooms. We all had started using Instagram over the summer and figured that there wasn't a platform that nicely collaged your photos effortlessly, thus we created it.

» **How did you get started?**

We literally drove straight back to our dorms from lunch, bought the domain and started drawing out the work flow for our product and website. Two weeks later, we launched our product.

» **What were the biggest challenges that you encountered?**

The biggest challenge that still continues on today is having the perseverance to continue taking risks and try new ideas out even after facing rejection several times.

» **What would you say is your greatest accomplishment along on the way?**

I think our greatest accomplishment has been our collaborations. I believe we've made great friends along the way that we'll continue to work with in the future. We've learn different processes and also gotten advice from industry experts along the way.

» **How did you get into this job? How easy or difficult it was for you to venture into this business?**

We got this job because we created it and followed our passions! It was both easy and difficult. It's easy to say you want to do it, but the difficult part was to actually start it and continuously pursue it and be willing to commit time and resources towards the legal paperwork and also technical infrastructure.

» **Have you always been interested in this kind of work?**

I've always been a fan of entrepreneurship and loved being educated about the tech eco system. However, I only recently became very interested in start-ups after interning at one last summer and saw that I enjoyed the working environment and thought process.

» **What has this experience been like? Any interesting points you would like to share?**

The experience has been amazing. It's been challenging, difficult and rewarding at the same time. There are good days and bad days, just like any other industry - but the amount that i've learnt in the past 7 months has been incredible and I don't think I would have grown or gotten this experience anywhere else.

» **What is the most challenging part of your job and why?**

I think my most challenging part is always putting my best foot forward. My two co-founders have put in an endless amount to create and style the website and product so I often feel like i'm letting the team down if I don't put time into the project. Also, every hour we take off from the project, our competitors are putting towards their product.

» **What fulfillment do you get from your job?**

The ideation process has been the most fulfilling, - being able to wake up with an idea and have the skill set (or someone in the team has the skill set) to bring the idea to life by the evening.

» **What important lessons have you learned in the process of establishing your company?**

That trust, communication and being responsible are the most important aspects of maintaining a stable company.

» **What do you think helped you the most in your success?**

I definitely think the support - whether from family, friends or random fans - has shown that our product does have a purpose and a target market, that our time and energy is worth it, to someone.

» **Where and how do you see yourself five or ten years from now?**

Hopefully still pursuing something I love and being creative.

» **How do you spend money – business or personal-wise?**

Pretty cautiously!

» **What is the most important advice you would give to other entrepreneurs?**

Find people that inspire you and always be willing to take the jump, you never know where you'll end up. It's not meant to be easy, if it was, everyone would do it.

www.posterfuse.com

@StephSLChan

www.facebook.com/posterfuse

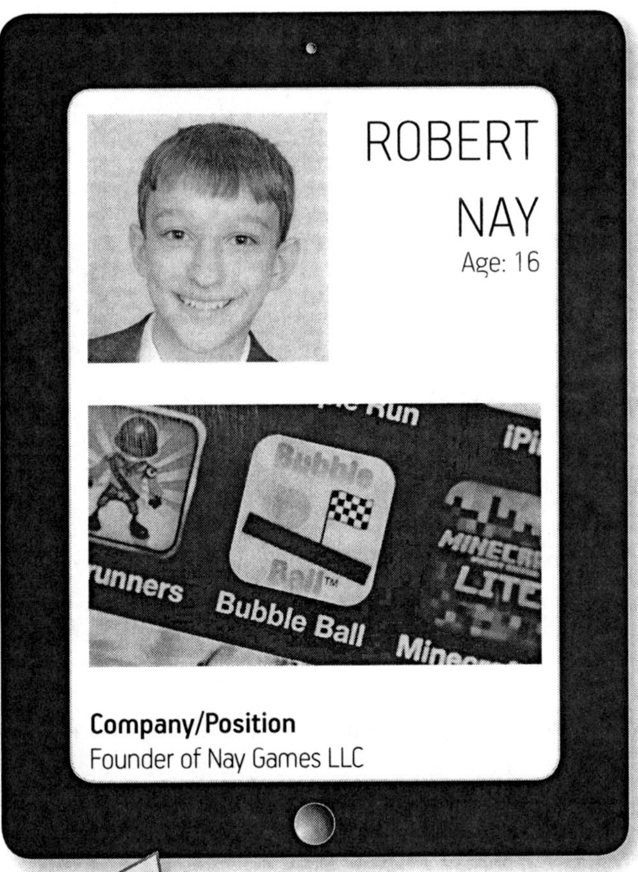

This 15-year-old computer genius programmed Bubble Ball, a mobile game that's had over 10 million downloads. Roberts first game also knocked the monster hit "Angry Birds" out of the number 1 most downloaded free game spot in the Apple app store. Robert is a successful young entrepreneur and has started his own company, Nay Games. Nay Games LLC is a leading mobile app creator.

» **Give a detailed description of the work that you do. What are your job responsibilities?**

I do a wide variety of things. Coding is what I mainly do and enjoy most, but I also do things such as level design, graphic design, testing, writing marketing copy, and whatever other odd jobs come up.

» **What made you think of your idea?**

I don't think there was one thing that made me think of my idea. After deciding on making a game, I wanted to use physics in it, and various things helped shape the idea from there.

» **How did you get started?**

During the summer of 2010, someone sparked the idea in me of making a mobile app. From there, I explored different possibilities and eventually created Bubble Ball.

» **What were the biggest challenges that you encountered?**

The biggest challenges I had were probably getting things set up for publishing to the iOS App Store, and when I ran into a coding problem that I couldn't figure a solution out for.

» **What would you say is your greatest accomplishment along on the way?**

Just getting a finished app onto the App Store for others to download. That was my goal, and doing that brought me a great sense of accomplishment. Yes, the app did proceed to get 16 million downloads, but I feel I didn't really have a part of that, and isn't so much something that I personally accomplished.

» **How did you get into this job? How easy or difficult it was for you to venture into this business?**

I got into this job because I created this job. Overall, it was fairly easy for me to get into this, particularly because it's both a small business and an internet-centered one.

» **Have you always been interested in this kind of work?**

I've been interested in computers and programming since I was very young, but Bubble Ball was my first endeavor with mobile development.

» **What has this experience been like? Any interesting points you would like to share?**

It's been crazy and a lot of fun. I've learned so much and had a lot of really neat experiences. The craziest part was probably the week where Bubble Ball rose to the #1 app and overtook Angry Birds Free.

» **What is the most challenging part of your job and why?**

I think the most challenging part for me is doing lots of things that are outside of my comfort or knowledge zone. I've always been a quiet and shy guy, so suddenly being on national media was, to say the least, different for me. Quickly coding a new feature or finding a pesky bug and submitting an update the next day was something that also challenged me.

» **What fulfillment do you get from your job?**

I think the most fulfilling part of this 'job' is seeing something that I made being played by millions of people. It's scary, but it's also fulfilling to me.

» **What important lessons have you learned in the process of establishing your company?**

That it's important to have fun. The whole reason I did this was as a hobby, just for fun. If there came a point where I was getting stressed out, I would need to take a step back and remember why I was doing this. I also learned to be open to all ideas, and that little details are important, even critical.

» **What do you think helped you the most in your success?**

Others. Whether it be people answering a question on the forums or a family member testing a new feature, I couldn't have done this without the help of others.

» **Where and how do you see yourself five or ten years from now?**

I hope to attend a local university. I'm not sure what I'm going to major in, but most likely it will be something computer or technology-related. Money that I've saved from Bubble Ball will help me to do that.

» **How do you spend money – business or personal-wise?**

Right now I'm mostly saving for college and other future plans. Business-wise, there's not really much aside from web hosting, developer, and software renewals

» **What is the most important advice you would give to other entrepreneurs?**

I'd say to just go out there and try things; you'll never know what could happen.

 www.naygames.com

 @naygamesllc

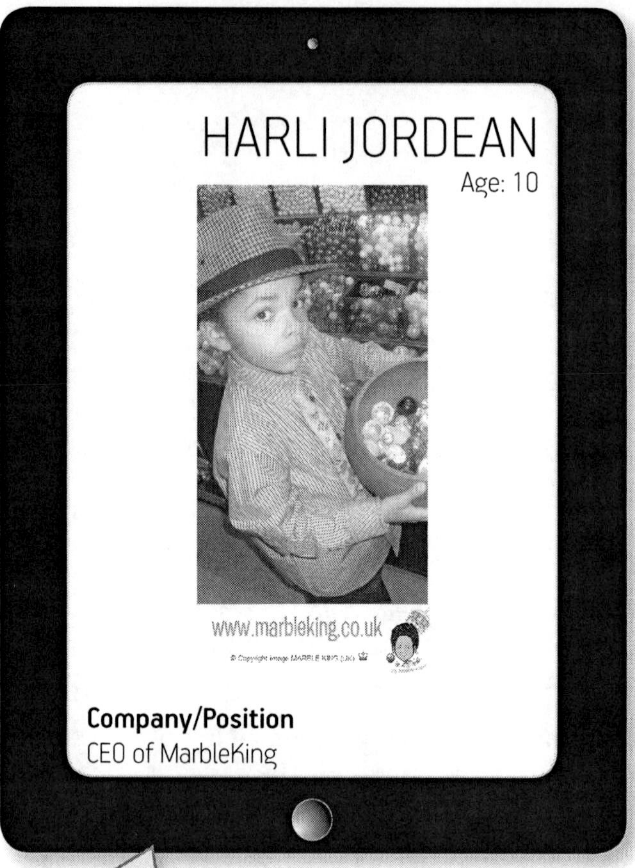

In 2011 Harli was noted as the Youngest CEO in the world at the age of 8. Harli is quite an impressive entrepreneur. He also set a world record, though technically he was the youngest CEO in the world when he was just 6 years old, at this time it was decided to grow his business slowly on the back burner and keep it on the low so that he could gain experience over many years, and that is how his company was initially started.

I am and consider myself an very ordinary kid, and do all the ordinary everyday things just like and the same as all my friends, fun as well as education is an important part of my life (anyone who knows me will only know too well that I like a good laugh), but I really do take part in the process of running my company, deciding on what marbles and games I would like to stock, sell, go to suppliers, meetings, getting parcel off to the customers and discuss what the next step is to move the business forward and progress to the next level regarding the Marble King (UK) company and other ventures that I have planned and may undertake for my future ongoing career.

I never thought it would become so popular as to reach global popularity all around the world in such a short period of time – at times the demand and interest has been so high that we have been struggling to cope with the number of orders that have been flooding in, but I'm not complaining as we manage to fulfill all orders and kept our customer very happy, that's business... my business!

I sell affordable loose and tubs of the glass toys marbles for children up to a whopping £599 for a limited edition Duke of York solitaire tables for the adult market and marble enthusiasts and serious collectors.

My marble collecting was so big everyone started calling me the Marble King of Britain - so obviously it was the first and most natural name for my company, Marble King (UK), www.MarbleKing.co.uk

Now I'm fortunate and extremely lucky to have a successful website www.MarbleKing.co.uk that's been up and running for two years, which has gone on and gained global recognition in 2011.

» **How did you get into this business?**

It all started back in 2009 when I just become absolutely obsessed with marbles; I was just crazy about playing and collecting them all day and every day until it made good sense to take it a step further, hmmm...could it become a business for me, could I be a young apprentice?! Surprisingly yes.

I have been lucky enough to have been the inspiration of the forming of the Marble King (UK) Company, to which I inspired my Mum when ask after I was walking and talking marbles so much "would you like a marble website of your own" as she knew that my interest in marbles was huge as I had her many days and hours helping me search the internet and stores for all kinds of marbles, she said she will build a site of me and my brothers who will be behind the scene, silent co-partners to practice business and gain experience for my future...

and that was the begining, 1st the building of my website, setting it up as a real business and creating a visual shop front for my company, the rest is history.

» **Where and how do you see yourself five or ten years from now?**

My future looks bright at present and I feel it is just the beginning and first of what I hope to be many business ventures and adventures that I will be embarking on along the way, after all time on my side

My first Business, the Marble King (UK) company is now turning over thousands of pounds and demand for products is extremely high from the UK and many countries of the world, such as US, Brazil, Mexico, Taiwan, Poland, Greece, Italy, France, Egypt, Israel to mention just a few...most kids just love marbles!

www.marbleking.co.uk

@TheMarbleKingUK

www.facebook.com/marble.king

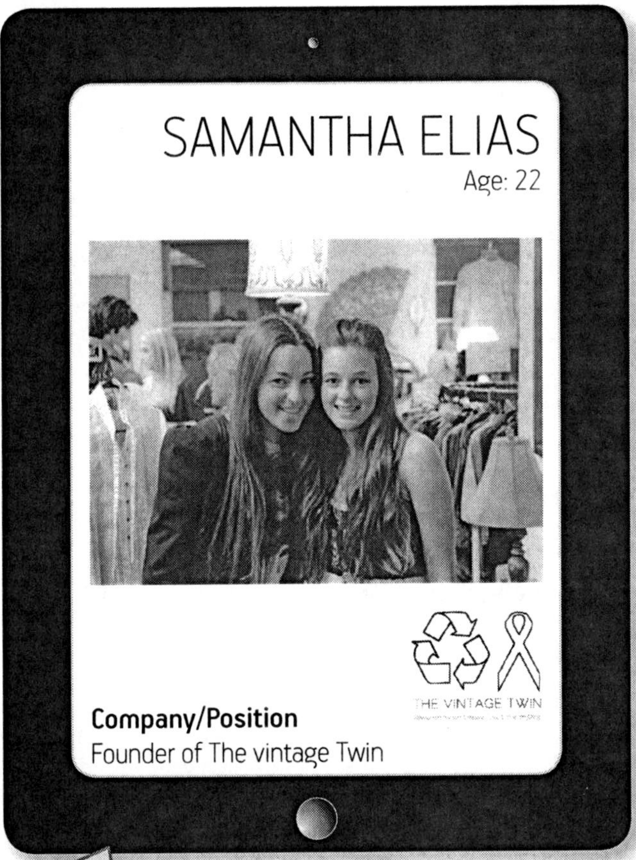

Samantha could not stand copy cat fashion or poor quality clothes that people spend way too much money on, so she decided to solve the problem by starting her own company with her twin sister. This young entrepreneur has a great taste for fashion and has successfully started a popular clothing company. The Vintage Twin (TVT) sells Hand-Picked, Reworked, and Original Designs in everything from apparel to home goods and beyond. When you get stopped about your TVT wears just remember that it's not just vintage, it's The Vintage Twin.

» **Give a detailed description of the work that you do. What are your job responsibilities?**

I run a company called The vintage Twin with my twin sister. We have been developing our website and building our inventory for it for about a year now.

» **What made you think of your idea?**

I studied sustainability and business in college and also got introduced to vintage clothing by friends in Michigan. When I brought my new hobby back to NY, people couldn't get enough.

» **How did you get started?**

Selling vintage t shirts in a trunk show in my mother's basement.

» **What were the biggest challenges that you encountered?**

Website development has been grueling.

» **What would you say is your greatest accomplishment along on the way?**

Owning and operating a storefront on campus for about a year. And then opening up a factory which employed 7 people full time. Also being able to sustain a business that donates 10% of proceeds to various charities at all times.

» **How did you get into this job? How easy or difficult it was for you to venture into this business?**

Easy to venture into but has been very trying to stay with given all the let downs and challenges.

» **Have you always been interested in this kind of work?**

I was always a business woman; I could not have imagined it would have been in second hand goods.

» **What has this experience been like? Any interesting points you would like to share?**

Confidence is important for hanging on when the outlook is grim, but proof of concept is more important. Balancing the two is an art and a necessity when starting and pursuing a business.

» **What is the most challenging part of your job and why?**

Planning is incredibly difficult when your business operations rely on the progress of something being developed remotely in uncharted territory. Partnering with my twin sister is as rewarding as it is challenging.

» **What fulfillment do you get from your job?**
A lot. People want our brand online!

» **What was it like when you realized you made your first million?**
Haven't yet but it's not far off. That is definitely not my driving force though I am itching for another opportunity to source in bazaars across Europe.

» **What do you think helped you the most in your success?**
Support from family and friends and passion about my brand.

» **Where and how do you see yourself five or ten years from now?**
Sourcing vintage goods all over the world and running a reworking factory remotely- preferably on a yacht in ten years.

» **How do you spend money – business or personal-wise?**
On my business. Then more on my business. And also saving for a rainy day- in business.

» **What is the most important advice you would give to other entrepreneurs?**
START NOW! Field opinions from as many people as you can. Prove your concept in at least two very different cities. Then be patient. Be very, very patient.

www.thevintagetwin.com

@TheVintageTwin

www.facebook.com/VintageTwin

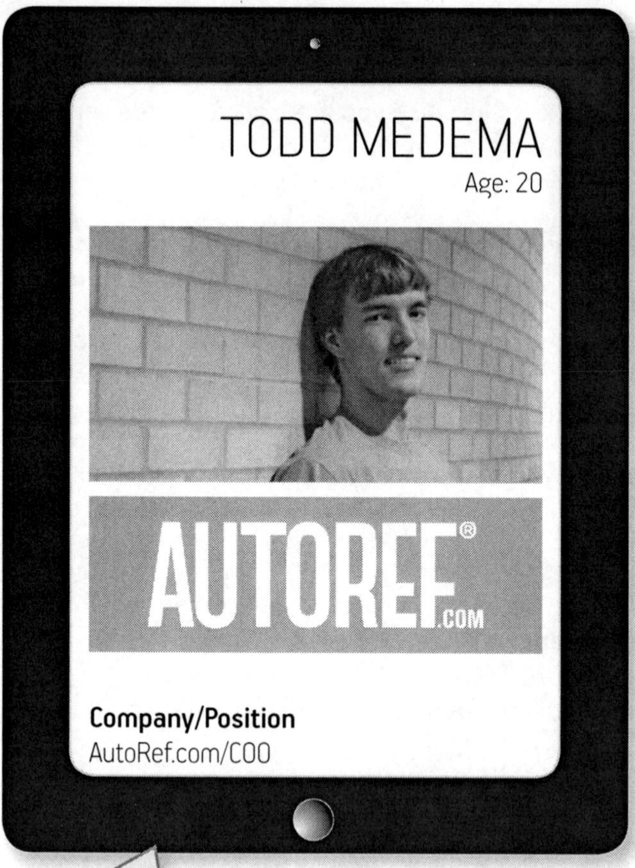

From California, this young entrepreneur started his first company his freshman year in high school and did not stop there. Todd wanted to make buying a car easier and less of a hassle for customers so he created something that would do just that. AutoRef simplifies car buying by providing information and reviews to consumers, then having dealerships bid for their business.

» **Give a detailed description of the work that you do. What are your job responsibilities?**

I'm the COO of AutoRef. While exact position definitions at small companies are a bit silly (since things change so quickly); my main focus is our employees - taking care of them and hiring more.

» **What made you think of your idea?**

The idea wasn't mine, it was our CEO's (Michael Pena) - he got it from working in the car industry for a decade. I firmly believe that worthwhile company ideas only come around from working in that industry for several years

» **How did you get started?**

For the first year, we holed ourselves up and built a first version of the website. Then, we gave it to customers and realized that we did everything wrong, and spent another 6 months rebuilding it. Only then did things start moving (but much of that time could have been avoided if we'd worked with customers from the start)

» **What were the biggest challenges that you encountered?**

First and foremost: finding good people to bring on your team. Our first designer was horrible, which was one of the main reasons we had to rebuild the site. Since then, we've brought on (and fired) other people that didn't mesh well with the team, or whose resumes seemed good but who failed to deliver

» **What would you say is your greatest accomplishment along on the way?**

Getting our team to where it's at now. Not only did we get an impressive amount of talent before we raised any real funding, but everyone on the team gets along amazingly

» **How did you get into this job? How easy or difficult it was for you to venture into this business?**

I met our CEO (who had the idea) through a fellowship I had. He was looking for a team, and I knew several programmer friends - so he brought me on as a manager/recruiter (as a freshman in college, no less!). Were I to do it again, I wouldn't pick the automotive industry, because everything is so slow-moving and resistant to change. Then again, that's also been a good thing because there's so much room and need for innovation!

» **Have you always been interested in this kind of work?**

I've always been interested in technology that makes a difference - I've never really cared what field it was in, so long as it was an interesting challenge

» **What has this experience been like? Any interesting points you would like to share?**

Running a company while in college has been interesting. It's certainly not for the faint of heart, and I believe it might be thoroughly overrated. You can't do college, or your company, justice. That being said, there are lots of entrepreneurial things you can do that have an impact but don't require all of the overhead of starting a company (clubs, side projects, etc)

» **What is the most challenging part of your job and why?**

The most challenging thing is finding good talent, for sure. If you want a company to be successful in the long run, it's not going to be about what you do now - it's about who you bring on the team, and what each of them does in the next 2-5 years

» **What fulfillment do you get from your job?**

Working with brilliant people. I've learned more talking with our programmers and designers than I've learned from any programming or design class in college

» **What was it like when you realized you made your first million?**

Well, that hasn't happened yet. But the more I think about the possibility, the more I realize that it wouldn't change much. If I blew it all on fancy cars, etc, then I'd be no better off than I am now. On the other hand, I could save it all, and use it to cover living expenses so that I could pursue side projects and passions - which would be really nice, but you also don't need anywhere near $1m to make that leap.

» **What do you think helped you the most in your success?**

You can't do anything meaningful alone. Making an impact is always harder than you expect it to be. Wait as long as possible to become an official company to avoid all of the bullshit overhead (taxes, lawyers, etc). Avoid investors at all costs, unless you need to grow at an insane rate. Product companies (ie selling toys) are easier than service companies (ie a web platform) because once you ship the product, you're done!

» **What do you think helped you the most in your success?**

My network. Knowing good programmers to hire, knowing experienced entrepreneurs to provide mentorship, knowing local investors to insure our acceptance to the local startup accelerator, etc

» **Where and how do you see yourself five or ten years from now?**

That's a good question. My current direction is to start a small products company with a friend that makes all sorts of interesting, random electronics. Then again, 5 years ago, I never would have seen myself starting AutoRef, so you never really know what opportunities will appear!

» **How do you spend money – business or personal-wise?**

Personally, I spend a huge portion of my money on technology and hobbies - things that I'm passionate about. Sure, it might be a bit silly to buy a $300 violin when I'm just getting started (and I'm learning to curb that excess), but not hesitating to make small purchases that I'll enjoy (such as an RC car or camera equipment) removes a lot of stress from my life, and keeps me focused on what new frontiers are possible. I'm also a HUGE fan of Kickstarter, because so many innovative, interesting ideas are cropping up there

» **What is the most important advice you would give to other entrepreneurs?**

Don't do it for the money. If you want money, get a corporate job, or work in Wall St - you'll make more money there. Start a company because you care about fixing something, or innovating. And before you start a company, find someone to start it with that you can trust, and who is smarter than you.

www.autoref.com

@ToddMedema

www.facebook.com/autoref

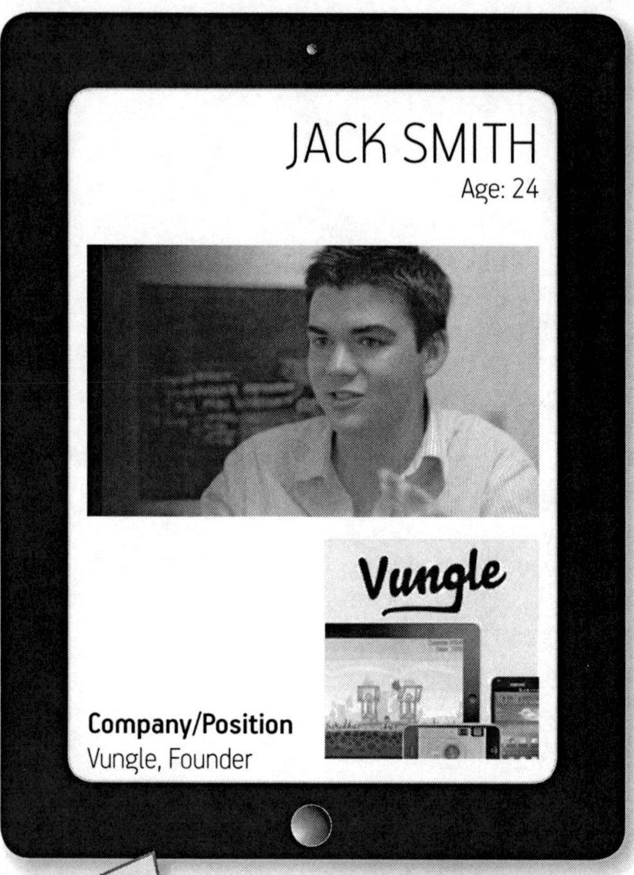

Jack is a determined and passionate young entrepreneur that is known for making things happen. Starting his company Vungle in London, he eventually made it to Silicon Valley. Vungle is a mobile video ad-network, powering some of the world's largest apps and games

» **Give a detailed description of the work that you do. What are your job responsibilities?**

Day to day I currently oversee product marketing; which involves surveying customer and team feedback as to the different products that we should be building; wireframing and drawing up Product Requirement Documents; making internal FAQs; handling support ticket systems etc.

» **What made you think of your idea?**

It evolved out of identifying a market need. The best ideas are as a result of seeing a problem and speaking to the people experiencing those problems.

» **How did you get started?**

I just started through the need and desire to start something. I've always worked for myself and can't imagine anything different than that.

» **What were the biggest challenges that you encountered?**

Raising funding through both our seed and series A rounds. Fundraising is very much about psychology and it took me a while to learn that.

» **What would you say is your greatest accomplishment along on the way?**

Getting into the AngelPad incubator program and moving out to San Francisco from London. It was a challenge getting here and a challenge once we arrived, but it's all made me more hungry for success.

» **How did you get into this job? How easy or difficult it was for you to venture into this business?**

It was hard work starting a company, but I wouldn't swap it for anything else.

» **Have you always been interested in this kind of work?**

Yes, I›ve always wanted to make my own money and be my own boss and have aimed to be entrepreneurial in everything that I do.

» **What has this experience been like? Any interesting points you would like to share?**

The experience has been amazing. I pulled some crazy marketing stunts to get into an incubator called AngelPad, that formed the basis of me moving out to San Francisco and then had to pull even more stunts to close our $2million seed round of funding.

» **What is the most challenging part of your job and why?**

I have new challenges every day, which is what's great about being an entrepreneur. A key challenge is to stay focused on what the top priorities are at any given time.

» **What fulfillment do you get from your job?**

Building something that has big impact and presence. I love seeing customers tweet about us on Facebook and the stories about how we've impacted people.

» **What was it like when you realized you made your first million?**

I didn't realize, it just passed by and things carried on as normal. I feel the same now as I did when I had $10 in the bank. I think it's important to stay grounded.

» **What important lessons have you learned in the process of establishing your company?**

Focus on surrounding yourself with great people and never give up. Also be slow to hire, bad cultural fits can have a massively detrimental effect on company morale.

» **What do you think helped you the most in your success?**

Never giving up, staying hungry and determined. It would have been so much easier to quit.

» **How do you spend money – business or personal-wise?**

Personally, I just buy random crap off Amazon. Business wise, I try to be very frugal, but we just spent a fair bit of money decorating the office. It can be hard to adapt to having millions of dollars in the bank that need to get spent to increase the speed of progress.

» **What is the most important advice you would give to other entrepreneurs?**

Go and do it. Don't wait until you're "ready". The best way to learn is by getting out there, making mistakes and then learning from those mistakes.

 www.vungle.com

 @_jacksmith

 www.facebook.com/vungle

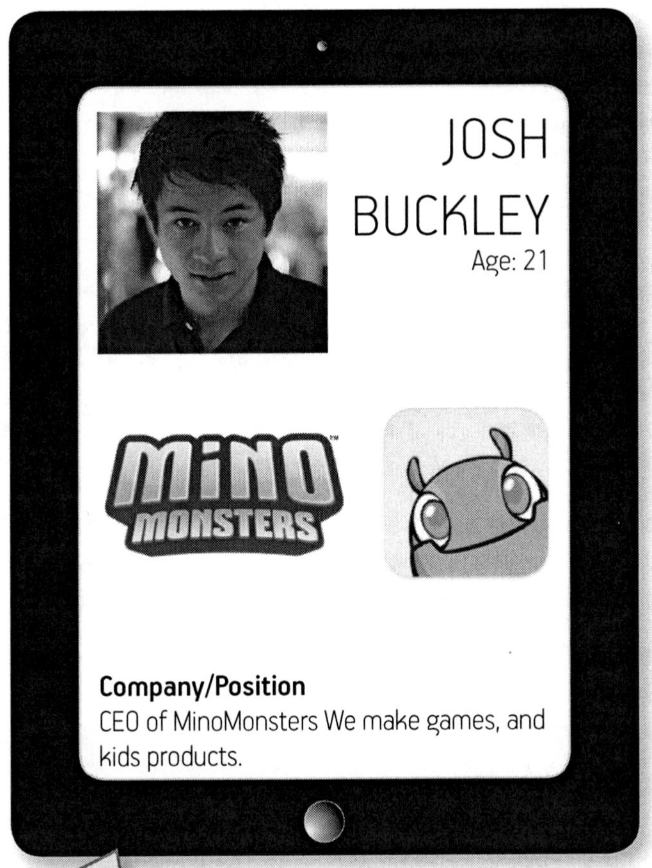

Josh Buckley grew up in Kent, England. At Age 15, he sold a start-up and began investing in other people's ideas. Josh moved to San Francisco, CA in 2010. Where he created Minomonsters and became the youngest person ever accepted into the Y Combinator, an influential start-up accelerator in Silicon Valley. Josh is now CEO of MinoMonsters. MinoMonsters is an adventure game founded by Josh for Apples devices. Monsters in your pocket! Collect your dream team of monsters and take them to battle, with online multiplayer. Each monster has its own special skills and personality, choose your team wisely. Collect, raise, and battle your way to greatness in this insanely addictive adventure game!

» **Give a detailed description of the work that you do. What are your job responsibilities?**

I am responsible for a few things, first and foremost making sure the company has enough money in the bank to run its operations. I make sure we are making money, hiring process, marketing process, investing process and more. I set the direction for the company. I manage all over, and make sure we are moving forward, and what we will do next.

» **How did you get started?**

I was in high school back in England, and I started building the game myself. I had started a company in the past so I had some money to start a company myself. I knew some investors in Silicon Valley in San Francisco, so I contacted them and then we spoke and after a few months I ended up raising 2 million dollars to start MinoMonsters.

» **What were the biggest challenges that you encountered?**

Managing people. Finding the right people and managing them well. Running a team and actually building a product that people want to use.

» **What would you say is your greatest accomplishment along on the way?**

Creating a product that millions of people use.

» **Have you always been interested in this kind of work?**

I have always wanted to create my own companies, so it has lead me down a path where I like to create games, and brands, so yes.

» **What has this experience been like? Any interesting points you would like to share?**

It's a lot harder than I expected, and everything takes so much longer, and it's defiantly more of a roller coaster of ups and downs than expected.

» **What is the most challenging part of your job and why?**

Making sure we are growing. Always making sure we are taking new opportunities, that's the most important thing to me, and it is hard because you are up against everyone in the market, you are up against the best, so make sure we are always growing.

» **What fulfillment do you get from your job?**

I have control over my life, I can do whatever I want, I have freedom, there is no one telling me what to do, I am creating something people all over the world love.

» **What was it like when you realized you made your first million?**

It's pretty cool, I don't really look back at it; I am always moving on to the next thing so I didn't waste much time thinking about it.

» **What important lessons have you learned in the process of establishing your company?**

Things are never as bad as they seem or never as good as they seem in a startup

» **What do you think helped you the most in your success?**

Surrounding myself with great people.

» **Where and how do you see yourself five or ten years from now?**

Running companies, hopefully running MinoMonsters as a much bigger company.

» **How do you spend money – business or personal-wise?**

Travel a lot, going all over, seeing friends.

» **What is the most important advice you would give to other entrepreneurs?**

You are the average of the 5 people you spend most of your time around, so pick wisely who you spend your time with and make sure they are people you look up to.

 www.minomonsters.com

 @joshbuckley

 www.facebook.com/MinoMonsters

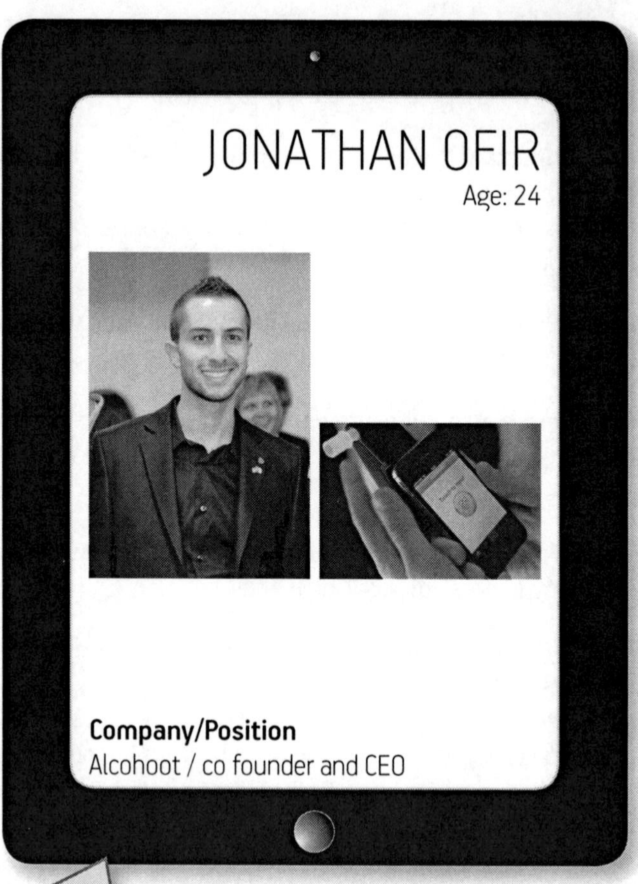

Jonathan and his partner are both former Israeli soldiers. While in the military this entrepreneur learned some wild statistics, that among military deaths more people die in accidents then in combat. This really struck him and he decided to do something about it. After the military and while in school Jonathan created his company Alcohoot. Alcohoot is a company that is developing the world's first smartphone breathalyzer. The Alcohoot system includes a small device that connects to your smartphone via Bluetooth. After a user breathes into the device, the Alcohoot app determines his or her blood alcohol content. It then provides some smart options for the user, depending on the level of alcohol in his or her blood, including phone numbers of local taxi companies and a "phone a friend" feature.

» **Give a detailed description of the work that you do. What are your job responsibilities?**

I double as the CEO and Head of Product Development so most of the work I do has to do with the creation of our hardware and our software and ensuring its quality and offers a killer user experience.

Since we are a small startup, the CEO role doesn't come as much in to play since we are just right before our first hire (up until now it was just the founders) and we make all decisions together.

» **What made you think of your idea?**

When my first partner Ben Biron and I were in the Israel Defense Forces we served in the Safety Unit. There we learned a lot about vehicular safety and a lot about drunk driving. It was that experience that led us to come up with Alcohoot.

» **How did you get started?**

At first we had no clue what we were doing, we had basically no technical knowledge and we needed to figure out how to build this software. The first thing we did was search for talented electrical engineers that could build this product. Luckily we found two amazing electrical engineers from Israel that took on this challenge together with us.

» **What were the biggest challenges that you encountered?**

The biggest challenge we had in the beginning was on the technical side. How do we build a breathalyzer? How do we connect it to the smartphone? What is needed to code the application?

There we so many technical questions that needed answering and knowing electronics was not enough - we needed alcohol sensor specialists and a whole bunch of other pieces to complete the puzzle. So I would say that was the biggest challenge initially.

» **What would you say is your greatest accomplishment along on the way?**

Our greatest accomplishment I think is that we brought the company to a very advanced stage and got amazing worldwide press while on a very very VERY tight budget.

» **How did you get into this job? How easy or difficult it was for you to venture into this business?**

It was difficult, I was a student when I started Alcohoot and I really never pictured myself running a breathalyzer company, ever. Eventually it all settled in and turns out the process and the type of work is really fun.

» **What has this experience been like? Any interesting points you would like to share?**

Taking the entrepreneurship route is the best thing I have ever done. It's also the hardest. I've learned so much running this business that I never learned in the classroom.

I think the most interesting thing about running an early stage startup is that the toughest thing is going to be emotions. You go into it thinking that money or technical obstacles are going to be the hard thing, but I've learned that the hardest thing is really keeping your emotions straight and fighting through the emotional roller coaster that is the start up world.

» **What is the most challenging part of your job and why?**

Keep everyone's emotions in tact while keeping myself sane. It's hard working around three strong personalities and it's a full time job just to keep everyone in check and focused.

» **What fulfillment do you get from your job?**

It's a rush that is unlike any other. The process is amazingly gratifying, even if you fail initially, because if you keep working at it eventually success will happen.

» **What important lessons have you learned in the process of establishing your company?**

Make sure you choose the right people as your co-founders. The only reason this venture has become a success is because our team has such amazing chemistry, and we will stop at nothing to make the venture a success.

» **What do you think helped you the most in your success?**

The ability to take multiple hits and get right back up every time.

» **Where and how do you see yourself five or ten years from now?**

In five or ten years from now I see myself working on my second or third startup and traveling around the world to try and see as much of this planet as possible.

» **How do you spend money – business or personal-wise?**

Personally I spend money mainly on food, entertainment, and travel. I try to put my money on experiences and not so much on possessions.

» **What is the most important advice you would give to other entrepreneurs?**
Never give up, never surrender.

 www.alcohoot.com

 @joniofir

 www.facebook.com/alcohoot

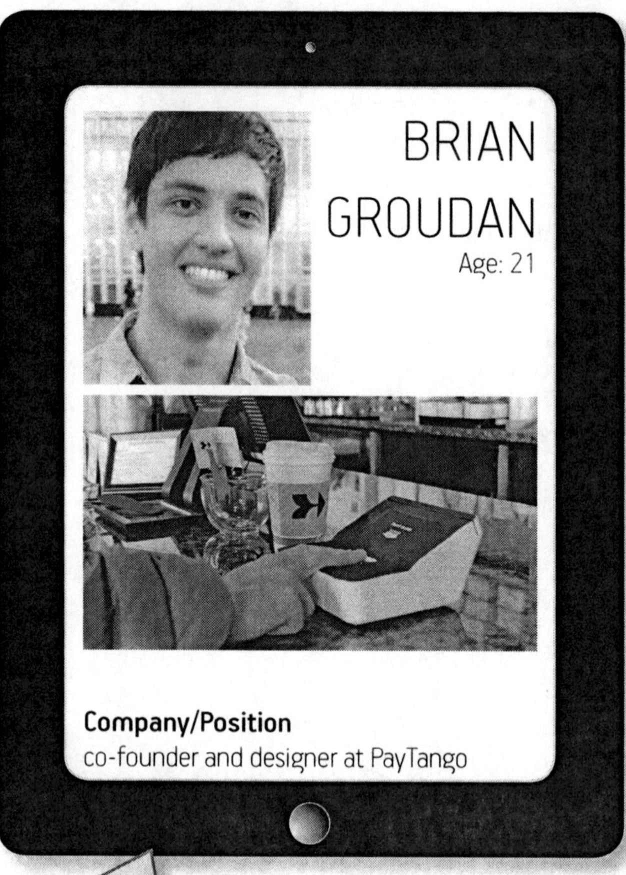

Wanting to solve the problem of always having to carry around all of your cards Brian and his partners created there company PayTango while in college at Carnegie Mellon University. PayTango allows you to pay with your fingerprints, linking your biometric information to your credit cards so you don't have to carry plastic ever again.

» **What made you think of your idea?**

Brian and his co-founders were initially interested in trying to help consumers "consolidate all of your cards into one card," I founded PayTango during my senior fall semester while a student at Carnegie Mellon University. PayTango provides biometric identification as a service for payments and access control applications. PayTango can be used for everyday activities like paying for a morning coffee or critical scenarios like identifying patient's medical information in a hospital.

» **How did you get started?**

This all started as something my team and I built over a weekend at a hackathon. In December, PayTango received seed funding from Y Combinator, and I decided to graduate early with my team and move out to Silicon Valley to further product development.

» **What fulfillment do you get from your job?**

I feel lucky to be able to work on something I'm passionate about and have the support of family and friends.

» **What about the future?**

PayTango wants to raise seed round funding and make its devices more widely available. College campuses are an obvious focus are gyms and "places where you carry your life on a card."

» **What is the most important advice you would give to other entrepreneurs?**

I don't have any incredible wisdom for young entrepreneurs, but I think Ev Williams (co-founder of Medium, Twitter, & Blogger) said it best: (1) Work with amazing people. (2) Take on Big Challenges. (3) Focus. (4) Take Care of Yourself. (5) Love those Close to You.

www.paytango.com

@b_c_g

www.facebook.com/PayTango

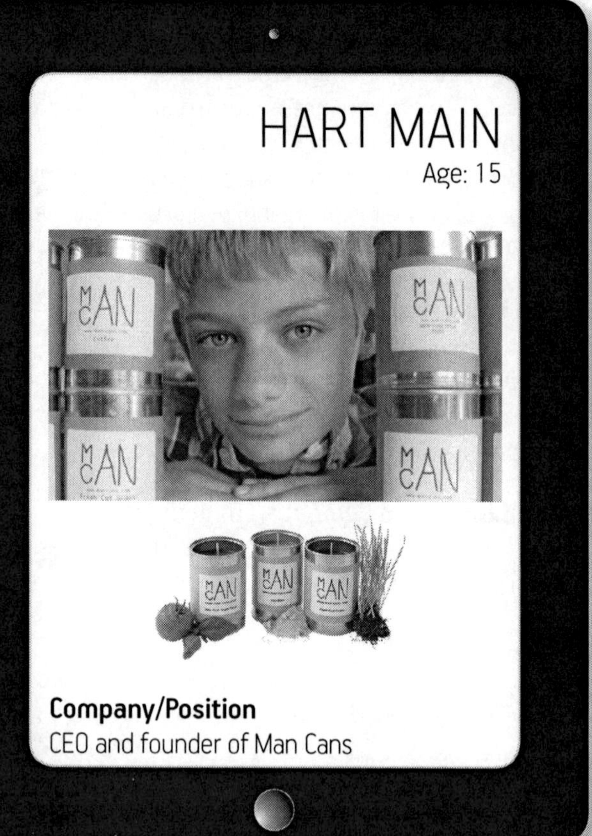

Hart was frustrated with most candles smelling like lavender, flowers, or fresh laundry and realized that there were no scents for guys. So he created ManCans. Man Cans are the one of a kind candle for men. With smells like fresh cut grass, grandpas pipe, sawdust, campfire, Memphis style barbeque, and much more. These candles are truly unique and delightful.

» **Give a detailed description of the work that you do. What are your job responsibilities?**

I oversee the production of the product and I am also in charge of making sure it runs smoothly.

» **What made you think of your idea?**

About 2 and half years ago my sister was selling candles for a school fundraiser and I thought why not make candles for men. I had the idea and I thought about what stuff I wanted, and I needed a container to put it in. I didn't want to use the glass jars because that is what every other candle is in. I thought why not use soup cans. As we started to get busier we decided to donate the soup to soup kitchens, that way we were helping people and still making a product.

» **How did you get started?**

At the time I had the idea we had no idea how to make candles. So we called a family friend who had a candle business and she told us where she got all her supplies from and started from there.

» **What were your biggest challenges?**

Some of the biggest challenges I face is being a kid and no one really taking me seriously, with my idea thinking it was my parent's idea and they were just using me for marketing purposes.

» **Where do you see yourself in 5 or 10 years from now?**

I would like to still be running this business or have sold the business to someone that keeps the charitable aspect of it; I would like to be in college perusing a career as a sports agent or sports marketing.

» **How do you spend your money business or personal wise?**

Most of the money that we make goes back into the business buying supplies. The original reason I started my business was I wanted to buy a bike, and I was able to buy a bike, and then the business started to grow.

» **What is the most important advice you would give to other entrepreneurs?**

The most important advice I would give is even if you have an idea for a business and have no idea or resources to start it. Like for me and candles and I didn't know how to make candles or any supplies to. Don't be afraid to ask someone you know or someone you don't know for help, because the worst thing they can say is no.

 www.man-cans.com

 @Man_Cans2011

 www.facebook.com/mancansohio

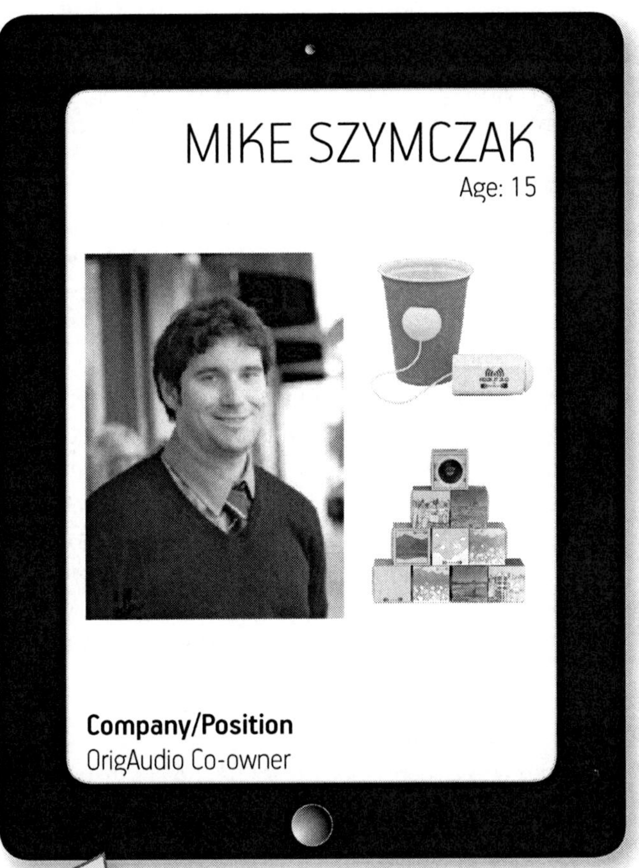

Mike is a bright and creative entrepreneur. Mike and his partner saw a need for portable speakers. This need came about from their own constant travels and desire for taking their music everywhere. He created his company when he was 25 and it has been a huge success. OrigAudio is an audio device company, with multiple products, headphones, speakers, and much more. Turn anything from a cup, trash can, tissue box to a dictionary into a speaker with Rock-It 3.0 (on left). They have speakers that are self powered, portable, and are recycled! They come in different designs and even have a blank one you can design (on right)! This is the ultimate audio company!

» **Give a detailed description of the work that yo u do. What are your job responsibilities?**

Manage production, order flow, fulfillment and operations. work on product development. handle in-bound sales and custom projects

» **What made you think of your idea?**

It was out of necessity. Tired of lugging bulky audio players around on business trips while working for JanSport, the duo started futzing with the idea of putting speakers into Chinese-food takeout boxes. The boxes start flat, and "whenever you want to use it, you pop it up," Lucash says. The idea sounded good. The product? Not so much. They moved on to putting a very old idea--origami--to work. In 2009, with $10,000 in seed money from Lucash's mom, the two launched OrigAudio (origami + audio) with one product: speakers, made entirely from recycled materials, that come flat and fold together. "The Chinese takeout box concept inspired us, but origami is what powered us," Lucash says. The two were selling 15 pairs a day through their website when the U.S. Marines placed a whopping order for 50,000 (launching OrigAudio's corporate gift division). Shortly after, Time waved its magic «best» wand. With the holidays coming on fast, the company quickly sold out of its stock of 25,000 units. That›s when Lucash and Szymczak gave their two-week notice to JanSport.

» **How did you get started?**

We started making a bunch of different prototypes trying to nail down the perfect size, sound, and ability to make it 'pop' up with the accent art of origami, hence our company name OrigAudio

» **What were the biggest challenges that you encountered?**

The biggest challenge was starting a business during one of the worst recessions of modern US financial history. To combat that we had to develop a product that would be affordable to the masses.

» **What would you say is your greatest accomplishment along on the way?**

TIME MAGAZINE TOP 50 INVENTIONS OF THE YEAR, ENTREPRENUER MAGAZINE'S ENTREPRENUER OF THE YEAR (emerging category).

» **How did you get into this job? How easy or difficult it was for you to venture into this business?**

It was very difficult to venture off on your own. It is such a risk and a plunge of faith to take off for your own business. For this particular business - it was certainly new to me as I did not have much experience in the electronics field as I was coming from event marketing.

» Have you always been interested in this kind of work?

Since I was about 15 or so I knew one day I would start my own business, never in 100 years did I think it would be in the electronics field - nor have the stellar and early success it has had.

» What is the most challenging part of your job and why?

The most challenging but the most exciting. It's the unknown that's challenging but exciting at the same time. Every day is different. Which is great because I never wanted to be in a monogamous type of work that is the same thing every day, it just doesn't fit my personality.

» What fulfillment do you get from your job?

A great deal of fulfillment. When I see somebody with my product, I know that not only do they enjoy their life but there listening to their music, and we are the prevayers of that enjoyment, and it just feels amazing inside to know that their using our product to enjoy their life and listen to their music. That and also being able to help out other young entrepreneurs and help them grow their business idea. Helping others is another thing we really focus on, so it's a fulfillment for both sides.

» How did you earn your first million? How long did it take? What was your reaction when you realized that you were a millionaire?

Completely shocked. When you start a business obviously your goal is to make money. With all the hard work and dedication that we put into this company it was just really fulfilling but shocking it had come to be at least a million dollars in sales, a million dollar valuation company. it was really shocking but at the same time internally proud of myself and Jason can say the same of the accomplishment of reaching that number, it is a significant number in any business early in the small business stage.

» What important lessons have you learned in the process of establishing your company?

You're going to hear no all the time. It's how you react that really sets apart the entrepreneur or the person that just gave it a try. The entrepreneur is going to get back up keep going, keep pushing, and not take that no to heart. For every one yes you hear nine nos. That and also to really take business very seriously but never take yourself too seriously.

» What do you think helped you the most in your success?

Hard work and dedication. I agree we got lucky on some things but I also think that you can create your own luck through hard work, I truly believe that. Hard work will beat anything else in this world.

» **Where and how do you see yourself five or ten years from now?**

Probably have another business or two. Continuing to grow origaudio with our product line. We come out with about 3 or 4 products a year. So in about 5 years we should have a pretty solid line of audio products, and also be starting some other companies as well.

» **How do you spend money – business or personal-wise?**

Business wise we just keep reinvesting into new products, and the development of those new products, that's the only way a business is going to grow if you reinvest your profits into the company.

Personal wise I like going to sporting events, music shows, and I like traveling a lot as well.

» **What is the most important advice you would give to other entrepreneurs?**

You can't score if you don't shoot. You never want to be the person sitting back maybe 5, 7 years later after you had this idea, you're sitting on the couch and then you see the product or your idea on a TV commercial and then you're going to be sitting there like ahh I had that idea remember! Just act upon your instincts is what I would advice upon, and go for it. Especially if you are a young entrepreneur there's no better time, because you have no responsibilities, you really should just give it a try at a young age.

 www.origaudio.com

 @OrigAudio

 www.facebook.com/OrigAudio

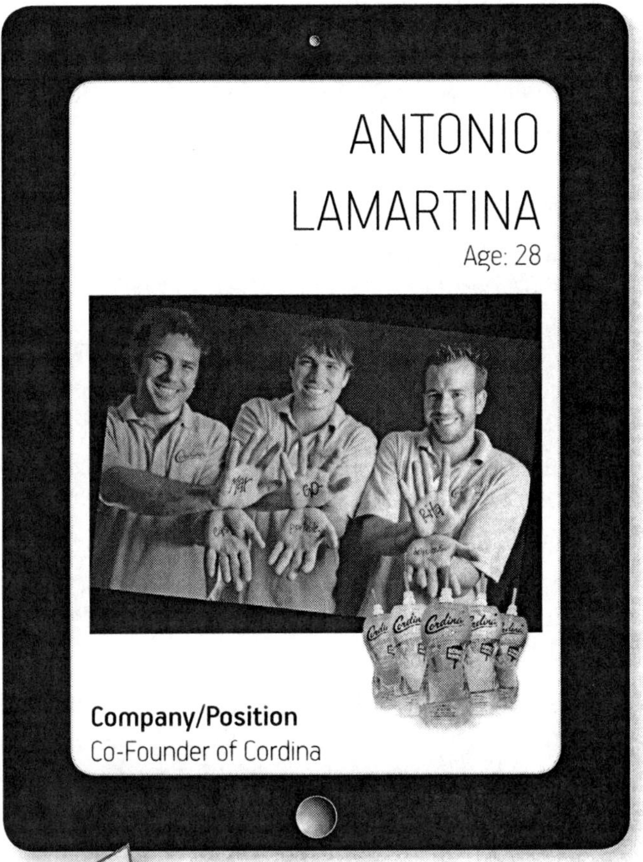

From New Orleans, Antonio is a smart and innovative entrepreneur. He thought it would be a good idea to make beverages for adults easier to bring on the go and places where you can't bring a blender with you. The business idea thought of by three friends is now distributed in national chains such as Wal-Mart, Winn Dixie, Dollar General, Walgreens, and Duane Reade. Cordina is an alcohol company, with cocktails on the go! The first juice box for grownups. These delicious drinks come in many flavors, and are great frozen or chilled. They are perfect for any occasion, if you are 21!

» **Give a detailed description of the work that you do. What are your job responsibilities?**

While all three owners share duties, my primary focus in on Sales. I travel approximately 60% of the time visiting with a wide range of wholesalers and grocery stores chains throughout the United States. My concentration is the daily's sales of the Cordina brand.

» **What made you think of your idea?**

Back in 2007, I was relaxing in Orange Beach, Alabama with my family. My mom asked me to make her a frozen cocktail. By the time I went to the kitchen, made it and brought it out to the beach, the frozen beverage had melted. I saw his nephew drinking a Capri Sun, and was struck with an idea. Why not make frozen cocktails to go? I called my older brother Sal, and that is when the idea was born. Why not make frozen cocktails to go? "Let's put booze in a bag," Antonio LaMartina told his older brother Sal LaMartina.

» **How did you get started?**

We started out by reading law books and understanding the in's and out's of the alcohol business. We started out in a small 2,000 square foot facility and hand filled over 100,000 pouches.

» **What were the biggest challenges that you encountered?**

Capital and Execution of the sales by the wholesalers. Since we self-funded the first couple of years, we had to limit overhead and everything was done by Sal, Craig and I.

» **What would you say is your greatest accomplishment along on the way?**

Walgreens National Rollout. Walgreens was out first National Retail account and they have been great partners since we started the company.

» **How did you get into this job? How easy or difficult it was for you to venture into this business?**

We just started it. We had little knowledge of the industry. It was near impossible to get started but we found a way.

» **Have you always been interested in this kind of work?**

No. I actually had no idea how this industry operated prior to starting Cordina.

» **What has this experience been like? Any interesting points you would like to share?**

The experience has been great, We sell Alcohol! We surround ourselves with good times!

» **What is the most challenging part of your job and why?**

Since the alcohol industry is regulated the three tier system, I would have to say Execution of sales by our wholesalers. We are a small supplier and it is very difficult to get their attention since the large supplier consume so much of their time.

» **What fulfillment do you get from your job?**

Every day I get to wake up, go to work with my friends, and sell alcohol. What more can I ask!

» **What was it like when you realized you made your first million?**

It was exciting to see our revenue over a million dollars as a company. We realized we were on to something. Now it is time to maintain our growth and fend off all the copy cats.

» **What important lessons have you learned in the process of establishing your company?**

You will make mistakes, just do your best to minimize them.

» **What do you think helped you the most in your success?**

Advice from Key strategic investors.

» **Where and how do you see yourself five or ten years from now?**

Still selling Cordina but in multiple countries.

» **How do you spend money – business or personal-wise?**

I don't! Conserve your money because you never know when a freight train will come through and take out your income.

» **What is the most important advice you would give to other entrepreneurs?**

Tell your friends and family about your ideas. Most people think that you should keep your idea to yourself, I disagree. Most friends and family are not here to steal your idea, they instead more than willing to help.

www.bigeasyblends.com

@DrinkCordina

www.facebook.com/CordinaFrozenCocktails

COSMAS OCHIENG

Age: 26 and married to wife Nelly

Company/Position

Ecofuels Kenya Ltd General Manager

Cosmas has been featured in Forbes 30 under 30, and is a truly inspiring entrepreneur. Eco Fuels Kenya is an East Africa for-profit social enterprise producing environment friendly biofuel, organic fertilisers, and plant health products from the nuts and seeds of the Croton Megalocarpus, a naturally abundant plant in East Africa with no other productive or commercial use.

» **Give a detailed description of the work that you do. What are your job responsibilities?**
Administration; Strategy execution, impact, and growth

Planning; Planning of production meetings, production activities, worker schedules, machine maintenance schedules and maintaining budget and product quality. Putting up of the supply chain management for feedstock collectors and for the supply of various feedstock materials to the factory,

Monitoring; Overseeing of the entire production system and ensuring that all the safety standards are being maintained and that workers are a biding by workplace safety rules

» **What made you think of your idea?**
I have passion about nature, especially plants, always interested in discovering new things that are contained in these plants that man can add value to and change lives

» **How did you get started?**
The business was founded on the opportunity presented by the untapped potential of the Croton Nut and the growing demand for locally produced clean energy and organic fertilizers. We thereby create significant social change from our operations and set an example of how social enterprise should be conducted in East Africa.

» **What were the biggest challenges that you encountered?**
Many people still did not believe that croton can be used for anything except for charcoal burning and therefore they continued cutting their trees for some time, this a bigger challenge. Another challenge was finance, since the machineries required were not available in Kenya at all.

» **What would you say is your greatest accomplishment along on the way?**
Every place that I have bought seeds, nobody has cut any tree, many people are planting trees instead, again I have been able to let people know the value in this indigenous tree which has been with them for decades.

» **How did you get into this job? How easy or difficult it was for you to venture into this business?**
During my study in the college, I did some research on oil bearing seeds and this was an eye opener in the benefits that can extracted from the plants which produce seeds.

» **Have you always been interested in this kind of work?**
Yes

» **What has this experience been like? Any interesting points you would like to share?**
There are a number of innovations that drive the Eco Fuels Kenya business model:

Our business is based on creating economic opportunity in an environmentally-friendly way from the nut of the Croton Megalocarpus, something that no other enterprise is doing on a commercial scale.

Our primary driver of business growth is organic fertilizer made from the Croton Nut and other indigenous inputs. We are the first producer of organic fertilizers in Kenya and are actively creating awareness and a market by educating small and large-scale farmers about the benefits of farming with organic inputs.

We collect all our raw material through a Seed Collectors Network made up primarily of BoP, rural communities who have little to no opportunity to generate income. By making the Seed Collectors Network the source of our raw materials, rather than a plantation, we ensure that the success of the company is tied tightly to the benefit of our local communities and our environment.

Because these innovations are core to our business model, we ensure that environmental and community impact are always at the forefront of our minds when making business decisions and growing our enterprise

» **What is the most challenging part of your job and why?**
After validating a market demand that exceeded our capacity to produce, the main challenge that lies ahead is sourcing enough raw materials (i.e. Croton Nut) in order to produce enough products to meet this demand. EFK, along with the NGO partners we are establishing in the Laikipia district, are confident that there is enough Croton Nut in the area, but the challenge is identifying exactly where the densest populations are, predicting when nuts will be falling and educating/organizing rural communities on the income generation potential of harvesting and selling the Croton Nuts to EFK.

» **What fulfillment do you get from your job?**
Creating an economic opportunity, without deforestation, out of an indigenously growing plant that has no other commercial use.

Promoting reforestation by encouraging rural community members plant additional Croton Megalocarpus trees to be harvested for income in future years.

Production our products without chemical additives or processes, creating no waste and consuming minimal amounts of electricity and water

Selling and promoting organic products that have a positive impact on the environment in replenishing soils that have been damaged by chemical fertilisers and reducing the amount of carbon emissions through the use Croton Nut Oil instead of traditional diesel fuel

» **What was it like when you realized you made your first million?**
It was a dream come true.

» **What important lessons have you learned in the process of establishing your company?**

Determination of the objective: The basic problem behind the establishment of a new company is the determination of the main objective.

Development of an idea: The entrepreneur develops the idea of starting business opportunities. He may visualize the business idea from himself or borrow from some experts.

Product analysis and market research: While selecting the nature and the type of business, one has to decide the types of product to be produced or purchased and the type of market needed.

Selection of forms of organization: After selection of the product and the type of market, the next problem I realized is the selection of the form of an organization. There are various forms of organization like sole trader, partnership, company and co-operative form of organization. The selection of suitable form of organization depends on nature and size of business, the amount of finance available and the managerial needs.

Selection of business Site: Selection of site include plant location, plant building and equipment and lay-out-for the plant. These factors are essential for the smooth conducting of the business.

Completion of legal formalities: I had to complete all the legal formalities at the time of starting the business enterprise. Something to note is that these formalities differ from organization to organization.

» **What do you think helped you the most in your success?**
My personal experience in processing plants having spent 5 years working

on natural oil production, including the past 2 years with a local NGO working on natural Resources Management.

Business Plan; So simple but outlines all of my business operations, including personnel needs, all budgets, sales and marketing procedures, manufacturing processes and revenue projections. I spent quite of time developing my business plan and got input from people with experience in biofuel and fertilizer industry.

Location; My location has given me upper hand in two perspectives, there are heavy distribution of croton tree which provides stable of feed stock supply, secondly many farmers are in the area for both flowers, horticultures and open farms.

Cost Control; I have managed to keep all by overhead costs under control, including manufacturing, advertising and location operations.

» **Where and how do you see yourself five or ten years from now?**

Developed and refined our core product line of organic fertilisers, plant health products and biofuel

Validated market opportunity by developing our B2B and retail distribution network of product sales

Sales of every product category exceeded our capacity to produce in our current years,

Doubled the size of our seed collectors network, contracting with 500 agents employing roughly 3000 rural community members to harvest 100 tons of Croton Nuts

» **How do you spend money – business or personal-wise?**

Business, Personal and charity work, I work with a young widows group that I founded in the year 2010 and registered the same year, currently they are 20 in number.

» **VISION**

The Group (New Hope Widows Group) strives to unite, develop and empower all young widows within the whole district in the creativity and innovative field into an organization that will provide dynamic widows' stability and that will transform, develop and support widows in solving their life (family) problems easily like any other woman in the community. To help widows secure and enjoy their inheritance rights such as land and other properties that belonged to the diseased husband.

» **MISSION.**

The Group advocates and supports the stability of widows. To this end, the Group represents the interests of, and seeks to promote the welfare and development of, widows, orphans and destitute children.

» **What is the most important advice you would give to other entrepreneurs?**

"It doesn't matter how many times you fail. It doesn't matter how many times you almost get it right. No one is going to know or care about your failures, and neither should you. All you have to do is learn from them and those around you because all that matters in business is that you get it right once. Then everyone can tell you how lucky you are." I was born from a very humble family that I didn't even how to begin life. I have done several things like; bicycle repair to fund my high school education, construction, selling clothes in the slums of Nairobi. I have come to know one thing, better future of every one lies ahead of him/her and never behind.

www.ecofuelskenya.com

KEVIN PETROVIC

Age: 19

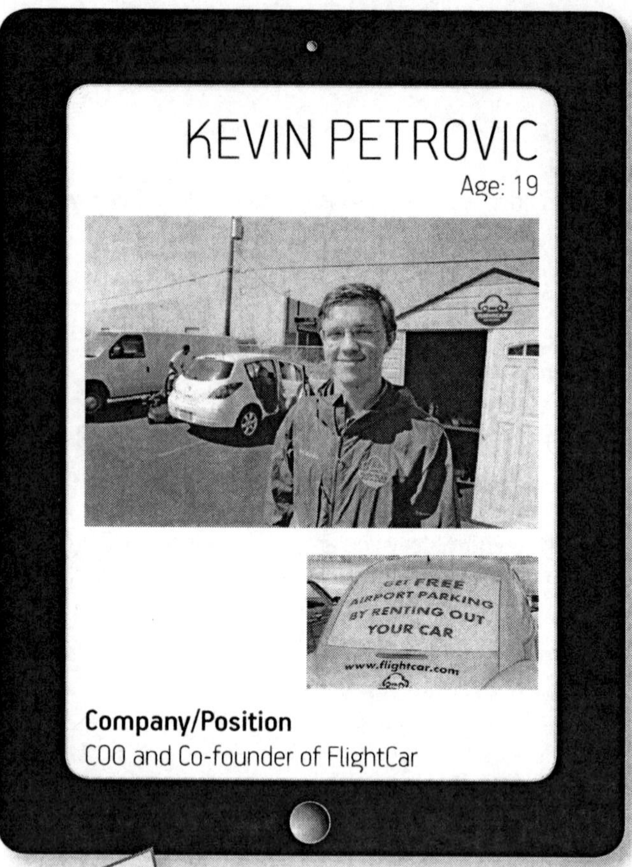

Company/Position

COO and Co-founder of FlightCar

Kevin created a cost effective way for people to park and rent cars. Starting his company as a teenager FlightCar lets people parking at the airport rent their vehicles out to other travelers. Every rental is insured up to $1 million, and every renter is pre-screened.

» **Give a detailed description of the work that you do. What are your job responsibilities?**

I generally manage the day to day operations at our locations and make sure that everything is running smoothly and without problems. This mainly means making sure everything is ready for customers before they arrive and being able to deal with problems quickly.

» **What made you think of your idea?**

We realized there was a huge inefficiency in the airport parking and car rental markets. Just look at the airport - there is one parking lot with all the rental cars, and one with all of the long term parking. We are trying to merge the two.

» **How did you get started?**

We started by attending an accelerator program in Cincinnati called the Brandery. We (the founders) had run businesses before but nothing quite like this, involving lots of employees and intensive day to day operations.

» **What were the biggest challenges that you encountered?**

In the beginning, it was a little tough to convince people that we were serious, given our ages. It was also a bit difficult to raise our first round of funding to get the operation started. Both of those issues were solved with perseverance though.

» **What would you say is your greatest accomplishment along on the way?**

We are proud of the fact that we are so flexible and dynamic at solving problems, and that we were able to go from Day 1 to launch in just about half a year.

» **How did you get into this job? How easy or difficult it was for you to venture into this business?**

We thought the time was right for a company like this. The first steps were hard - we had no idea what to do - but as we started making progress it got easier.

» **What has this experience been like? Any interesting points you would like to share?**

It has definitely been a learning process all the way - and it really continues to be.

» **What is the most challenging part of your job and why?**

A lot of the time we are flying blind - this is mostly because we are figuring out the business as we go along. I may have one goal in mind but along the way, I discover that there are actually 10 intermediate steps and things that need to be done before I can reach the final goal. It is definitely frustrating, to say the least.

» **What fulfillment do you get from your job?**

It is amazing to know that we are running a service that so many people enjoy and use. We strive to make sure that each person that uses FlightCar comes out of the experience extremely satisfied.

» **What was it like when you realized you made your first million?**

With startups, the money is only on paper - you make money based on the "valuation" of the company. So, while in theory, my stake may have had a 7 figure worth, it is certainly not cash value. For that reason it wasn't a big deal - I just chuckled and mentally noted it down.

» **What important lessons have you learned in the process of establishing your company?**

One thing I have started to do a lot more of is plan far ahead. I used to do this even before but the scope of it is much larger. I make clear timelines for getting a large project done - operationally. A lot of major changes I make require significant planning and execution steps.

» **What do you think helped you the most in your success?**

For me this was a particularly hard thing, but sometimes just accepting that you're wrong is hugely important in ensuring you make the right choices and make the right moves.

» **Where and how do you see yourself five or ten years from now?**

That's way too far out to tell! While most people think in years, I think in an order of magnitude smaller - in months.

» **How do you spend money – business or personal-wise?**

When I do have free time, I really enjoy taking trips to other parts of the world. The more exotic and off the beaten path, the better. It feels really genuine when you're the only tourist at a particular location.

» **What is the most important advice you would give to other entrepreneurs?**

Don't be afraid of taking risks. There is an old Slovak saying: "risk je zisk" - basically, "risk is rewarded with gain". This is not always true, of course, but the biggest gains are made by taking big risks.

 www.flightcar.com

 @FlightCar

 www.facebook.com/flightcar

KELLEY COUGHLAN

Age: 25

Company/Position
Melrose PR (owner) www.melrosepr.com, and Pursecase (co-founder)

Kelley is a sophisticated young entrepreneur who has already accomplished many great things. Kelley and her partner were tired of digging around a purse to find their phones, so they created something to fix that. Pursecase is a unique yet genius way to carry around your iphone in style. Kelley also owns Melrose PR, an LA based boutique Public Relations firm. Melrose PR specializes in a combination of both new media and traditional PR for the health, beauty, travel, hospitality, fashion, and consumer product industries.

» **Give a detailed description of the work that you do. What are your job responsibilities?**

*For Melrose, I manage the company, oversee all the hiring, acquire new clients, pitch new business, and manage the day-to-day upkeep of all the accounts

*For pursecase, Jenn and I split all the responsibilities up... but between the two of us we do all the design work, business management, marketing, PR, and we oversee all the distribution and production.

» **What made you think of your idea?**

*For Melrose- my background was working in PR at various different boutique agencies, so it was a natural progression

*For pursecase- it was out of need. We wanted something that we could use at events that would help us to not lose our phones.

» **How did you get started?**

I started by doing PR as a freelance publicist, working with just a couple clients. As the demand grew, I thought it would be beneficial to start forming an agency so that I could scale the business and create a brand.

» **What were the biggest challenges that you encountered?**

*For both- raising capital and drafting the business plans

*For pursecase- finding a manufacturer to create our product

» **What would you say is your greatest accomplishment along on the way?**

Creating a unique product, and taking it from just an idea all the way to an actual product on the market.

» **How did you get into this job? How easy or difficult it was for you to venture into this business?**

For PR- I interned at various different PR firms

» **Have you always been interested in this kind of work?**

*Pursecase- no! If you had asked me a year ago if I was going to produce and sell iphone cases I would have laughed at you!

*Melrose- I became interested in PR while studying at USC in the Annenberg School for Communications.

» **What has this experience been like? Any interesting points you would like to share?**
Melrose PR has been up and down

» **What fulfillment do you get from your job?**
It is most satisfying to work for yourself, and do what you love. In both, I love what I do and I feel that I am good at it, so it's fun and exciting. I love being able to mentor people also, which I do often through our internship program.

» **What was it like when you realized you made your first million?**
I haven't yet! PROB THIS YEAR! Fingers crossed.

» **What important lessons have you learned in the process of establishing your company?**
Everything takes longer than you think it's going to! Whether it's creating new samples for pursecase or signing with a new client for PR, it takes time and effort!

» **What do you think helped you the most in your success?**
Perseverance and drive.

» **Where and how do you see yourself five or ten years from now?**
Five years- Married, will have sold pursecase, hopefully pregnant and will be working at Melrose PR. Ten years- probably will have 3-4 kids by then.

» **How do you spend money – business or personal-wise?**
I try to spend my money on healthy food, I think keeping your body fit and healthy is important for maintaining a good outlook on life and to keep a good work/life balance. I like to treat myself to a nice new outfit every few months, and I like to get a massage once a month.

» **What is the most important advice you would give to other entrepreneurs?**
Never to be afraid to ASK for help or advice, and to listen to it. The best tips I got were from friends and colleagues.

www.pursecase.com
www.melrosepr.com

@kelleycoughlan

www.facebook.com/melrosepr

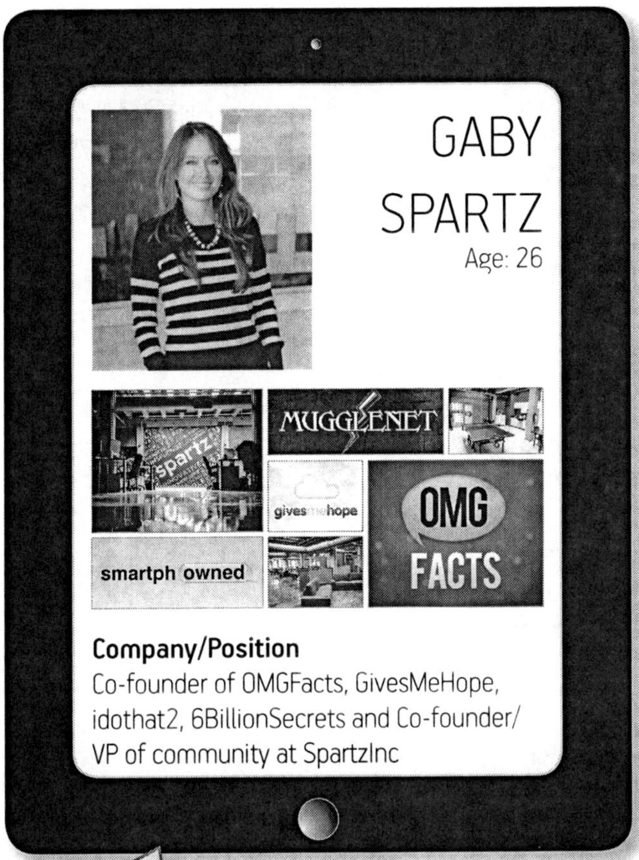

Gaby Spartz is a very smart young entrepreneur. She has been creating websites since a very young age and knows a lot about technology. Gaby and her husband Emerson founded a company known as Spartz Inc. They have developed predictive science to measure the viral potential of websites. They have a 90 percent success rate and millions of viewers every week.

» **Give a detailed description of the work that you do. What are your job responsibilities?**

Apart from being co founder of the company and having all of the stuff to do with that, my team specifically handles everything that is the constant moderation, social media management, and community management of our site. This includes launches of new products, launches of new books and apps, monitoring the content that comes out of our sites to make sure that everything is appropriate and good, and lastly promoting both our new sites and new products and using our existing resources to promote new developments in the company.

» **What made you think of your idea?**

I graduated in 2009, this is when the economy was getting really bad and it was tough being a senior getting out of school, so I couldn't get a job coming out of school, and I pretty much had a lot of plans to do nothing. In that period there was a site known as FML, it's a pretty funny site but allot of the stories are actually depressing. The first site on our network was called givemehope and it was launched as a response site to FML. Givemehope was a site where people shared inspirational stories instead of sad stories, and they could be happy about reading good things happening to great people, and it was received very well, and that is kind of what got the company started. It was the first site and it got everything else rolling.

» **What were the biggest challenges that you encountered?**

When this was not a job rather a hobby, it was difficult to manage because at the same time I was also trying to find a job and not really knowing if this is what I wanted to do for a living. Scaling was difficult for us because we started out as a small server, it was a smaller site, and I didn't have a developer. Dealing with increased numbers of people coming to our site and higher traffic and everything that comes with having a bigger network of websites, that was all challenging but we were able to overcome it.

» **What would you say is your greatest accomplishment along on the way?**

I would say probably being named to Inc. 30 under 30. It was a huge accomplishment. There are other awards but that one was very meaningful and it was meaningful for both me and my family, and it was nice confirming evidence for everyone else who might not necessarily understand what we were doing and at given times it was very nice to show them a big recognized magazine was recognizing our work.

» **How did you get into this job? How easy or difficult it was for you to venture into this business?**

It was pretty easy in the sense that when I was 12 I used to have a blog, it was a personal blog, and it was full of cute animals and stuff like that, because that was what I liked at the time. I taught myself to code when I was really young, just for fun. I went to school for business but I did not go into any tech related part of business. When I graduated and I was looking for jobs and not really knowing what to do, this was still something I did as a hobby, so it originally started out as something I was doing for fun so in that regard it was very easy because I was doing it because I enjoyed it.

» **What has this experience been like? Any interesting points you would like to share?**

One of the most rewarding things about what we do is knowing that we reach so many people and hearing those peoples feedback along the way. For some of the funnier sites people will say "I was really bored in class and I was happy I got to spend some time on your site and just laugh" that's meaningful but some of our other sites like the ones that people share their secrets or inspirational stories we've gotten stories about people who said they were going to commit suicide that day and stumbled on the site and they read it and regained hope and decided not to go through with it and continue giving life a chance. Even things like people saying they were considering dropping out of school and now they read it every day and its therapeutic for them, those are some of the most humbling things I have ever read. It's important to see how impactful something like this can be.

» **What fulfillment do you get from your job?**

Knowing that you are making difference on a large scale. It's always nice when you can do something for a friend but when you are doing something that impacts millions and millions of people, it's a really humbling experience.

» **What was it like when you realized you made your first million?**

I think at some point or at least for me, it was never about the money, and coming out of school the only thing I really wanted for it to work out and to make a whatever living, and that I didn't have to be doing accounting at some company. It was always about waking up in the morning and feeling like your making a difference and being motivated to come to work, and back then work wasn't even coming to an office, it was waking up and being on your computer.

» **What important lessons have you learned in the process of establishing your company?**

No matter what you are doing there is never a way to please everyone. That was something that I didn't understand before, or at least not on an emotional level. No matter what site were launching, even if it's the best site that we've ever launched, there's always people who have problems about certain things. At a certain point you have to stop and look at from the perspective of is this making a difference and is this helping people. Are there a couple people who might have issues with it? Yes, that's possible, but as long as you're overall doing it with good intentions and you're doing it because it's going to have a positive impact in the world then it's worth doing. It's just the nature of having so many eyeballs in whatever it is that you're doing somebody is going to have an issue about something.

» **What do you think helped you the most in your success?**

I would say 2 things. One is the fact that I was doing this with Emerson and we were doing it simultaneously really helped a lot because then you have someone you can rely on, somebody who's judgments you can trust, and someone who is putting as much work in as you are. When you have something that is a budding idea, it's very important to have something like that or someone you can count on and who understands the problems you have and the things you are trying to overcome. The second thing that helped was that I went to school at Notre Dame, and at Notre Dame they teach you very good work ethic. To the point where it's no longer am I even motivated to do work today, it's get up, do work, work all day. In the beginning there was no difference between weekdays and weekends, it was work, work, work, and being able to stay focused and motivated is very important and I think that is something that Notre Dame instilled in me early on.

» **Where and how do you see yourself five or ten years from now?**

That's a tough one, because times are always changing the same way in that if someone asked me 5 years ago if I would be doing this I would have no idea what to say. 5 years ago I was still in college and had no idea what I wanted to do after graduation. Times change a lot but I would like to see myself still working in something I know is having a positive impact on people's lives in some way shape or form. It might not necessarily be in the form of these websites, it might be something else but probably something with technology, that's something I've always been drawn too. It could be this network on an even bigger level then today, it could be anything the times to change too fast for me to give a concrete answer.

» **How do you spend money – business or personal-wise?**

Business wise we reinvest everything back into the company, most of the costs of running the company are the cost of labor, and hosting. We don't have very much overhead other than that. We always make sure to have a good office environment here, so we buy things like bean bags and hammocks, and we go on grocery runs to have food for everyone at the office all the time.

Personally I have a hobby that I'm ridiculously dedicated to. It's a strategy game. A card game called magic gathering that I play very competitively. A lot of my disposable income goes towards spending money on this hobby, apart from that food, and other random entertainment.

» **What is the most important advice you would give to other entrepreneurs?**

Talk to somebody who has more experience then you. I think that is extremely important. There are a lot of people who have business ideas and they might not be aware such a business already exists and is either A. successful or B. unsuccessful or C. had a lot of problems they've had to overcome. People are often concerned saying there idea to somebody, that people will run away and take their idea. Creating a successful company has nothing to do with whether or not you were squatting on an idea for 20 years. Most like somebody out there has thought of it, has tried it and succeeded or failed, so if you talk to people who have more experience then you or people in the industry or people who can give you pointers, you'll most likely find things that will either encourage you to continue with this business idea, or discourage you from doing it. But it is important that you find out what the situation is with this idea because it will most likely happen in some form.

www.spartzinc.com

@GabySpartz

www.facebook.com/SpartzMedia

ASYA GONZALEZ

Age: 16

Company/Position

Owner & Designer for Stinky Feet Gurlz

Asya started her company at age 14.Stinky Feet Gurlz is a company that designs, markets and sells 1940s-inspired t-shirts and apparel. Asya has also created a charity foundation, called She is Worth it, to bring awareness and action to the atrocious child sex trafficking industry, by donating a part of every sale to raise money to benefit victims of sexual assault.

» **Give a detailed description of the work that you do.**

I am the owner and designer for Stinky Feet Gurlz. My designs are Gurlz that are 1940's inspired with big red lips, long luscious lashes and adorable pin curls. I am the owner of She Is Worth It! A campaign to bring Preventative Awareness for Child Sex Trafficking and I'm also the creator and owner of Ask Asya, a teen advice segment for beauty, fashion and teen life advice.

» **What made you think of your idea?**

I have always been interested in fashion and have always known since I was a very young child that I wanted to be a Fashion Designer. I made a doodle that I took to my parents and they loved it so much they encouraged me to take it further and put it on t-shirts!

» **What were the biggest challenges that you encountered?**

Definitely not knowing a thing about owning a business. Not understanding how to buy in bulk or how to get a good price on printing. Small things like that can really frustrate someone just getting started. Another thing was getting negative feedback from ... believe it or not ... family members that the name of my company was too weird. I had to shrug my shoulders and keep going.

» **What would you say is your greatest accomplishment along on the way?**

I love everything I've done up till now but the biggest and best thing was being asked to join Independent Youth's as one of their public speakers. I get to do peer-to-peer entrepreneur presentations! I love it!

» **How did you get into this job? How easy or difficult it was for you to venture into this business?**

I do three things: Design tshirts, bring awareness to Child Sex Trafficking and run an advice segment. The only difficult thing was getting started, getting that first foot in the door.

» **What fulfillment do you get from your job?**

Getting emails from young girls saying I'm an inspiration! I just got one that said, "I will follow you anywhere!" How amazing is that?!

» **What important lessons have you learned in the process of establishing your company?**

To believe in myself. To believe in the skills I was born with and the ones I have developed. When I really began to believe in myself, my confidence levels really rose and I was able to stand in front of 500 students and speak about my experiences! When you have a skill, NO ONE can take that away from you!

» **What do you think helped you the most in your success?**

Hands down having parents who were encouraging as well as demanding. They demanded that I never give up, even when I was tired. My mom travels everywhere with me and I lean on her as well as learn from her. She's amazing and she gives me the energy to keep going and to keep dreaming. I'm allowed to dream!

» **Where and how do you see yourself five or ten years from now?**

I really see myself starting new and bigger businesses. I'm already working with my brothers on another venture. But as far as my designing, I see myself starting a couture line, still having Stinky Feet Gurlz and still working hard for those children caught up in the world of sexual slavery!

» **How do you spend money – business or personal-wise?**

I'm big on reinvesting the business money back into the business. Personal wise...I'm still learning! I'm a little impulsive so when I see something I want, I have been known to blow all of it on stuff. Which is BAD! I've started listening to Dave Ramsey to help me be smarter with my saving and spending choices. I'm just being honest here! LOL!

» **What is the most important advice you would give to other entrepreneurs?**

How important it is to build your own dreams. I read a quote once: "If you don't build your dreams, someone else will hire you to build theirs." How powerful is that?!

www.stinkyfeetgurlz.com

@stinkyfeetgurlz

www.facebook.com/Stinkyfeetgurlz

Conclusion

All of these stories are truly inspiring, and there are many more out there just like it. I have always been passionate about making things happen, and have always been encouraged by other people that do the same. I decided to put my own knowledge that I have learned from Universities, books, and my own businesses together, as well as interview tons of young entrepreneurs to put it all together and create this book, for other people to use as a tool, and learn from their advice. Remember to have courage, and not be afraid to ask for help or step out of your comfort zone. Be determined with anything you do and nothing can stop you. Surround yourself with positive, smart people, and create a successful environment for yourself. Keep your eyes open for opportunities when others see the ordinary. Find your passion and success will follow. Most importantly go out there and make it happen, because a great idea is nothing until you take action.

Now that I have given you the knowledge of what it takes to become successful in anything that you do. It is time for you to take action! Nothing is stopping you!

\ information can be obtained at www.ICGtesting.com
d in the USA
V07s1158051213
130BV00009B/499/P